T0259010

ADVANCES IN APPLICATIONS OF COMPUTATIONAL INTELLIGENCE AND THE INTERNET OF THINGS

Cryptography and Network Security in IoT

ADVANCES IN APPLICATIONS OF COMPUTATIONAL INTELLIGENCE AND THE INTERNET OF THINGS

Cryptography and Network Security in IoT

Edited by
Rajdeep Chowdhury, PhD
S. K. Niranjan, PhD

AAP APPLE ACADEMIC PRESS

First edition published 2022

Apple Academic Press Inc.
1265 Goldenrod Circle, NE,
Palm Bay, FL 32905 USA

4164 Lakeshore Road, Burlington,
ON, L7L 1A4 Canada

CRC Press
6000 Broken Sound Parkway NW,
Suite 300, Boca Raton, FL 33487-2742 USA

2 Park Square, Milton Park,
Abingdon, Oxon, OX14 4RN UK

Library and Archives Canada Cataloguing in Publication

Title: Advances in applications of computational intelligence and the Internet of Things : cryptography and network security in IoT / edited by Rajdeep Chowdhury, PhD, S.K. Niranjan, PhD.
Names: Chowdhury, Rajdeep, editor. | Niranjan, S. K., editor.
Description: First edition. | Includes bibliographical references and index.
Identifiers: Canadiana (print) 20210336048 | Canadiana (ebook) 20210336102 | ISBN 9781771889698 (hardcover) | ISBN 9781774638729 (softcover) | ISBN 9781003127482 (ebook)
Subjects: LCSH: Internet of things—Industrial applications. | LCSH: Computational intelligence—Industrial applications. | LCSH: Cryptography. | LCSH: Computer networks—Security measures.
Classification: LCC TK5105.8857 .A38 2022 | DDC 004.67/8—dc23

Library of Congress Cataloging-in-Publication Data

Names: Chowdhury, Rajdeep, editor. | Niranjan, S. K., editor.
Title: Advances in applications of computational intelligence and the Internet of things : cryptography and network security in IoT / edited by Rajdeep Chowdhury, S.K. Niranjan.
Description: First edition. | Palm Bay, FL : Apple Academic Press ; Boca Raton, FL : CRC Press, 2022. | Includes bibliographical references and index. | Summary: "This new volume illustrates the diversified applications of IoT. The volume addresses the issue of data safekeeping along with the development of a new cryptographic and security technology as well as a range of other advances in IoT. Advances in Applications of Computational Intelligence and the Internet of Things (IoT) looks at the application of IoT in medical technology and healthcare, including the design of IoT-based mobile healthcare units and a blockchain technique based smart health record system. Other topics include a blended IoT-enabled learning approach through a study employing clustering techniques, an IoT-enabled garbage disposal system with an advanced message notification system through an android application, IoT-based self-healing concrete that uses bacteria and environmental waste, an IoT-enabled trash-the-ash application that regulates flow, and more. The fresh and innovative advances that demonstrate computational intelligence and IoT in practice that are discussed in this volume will be informative for academicians, scholars, scientists, industry professionals, policymakers, government and nongovernment organizations, and others"-- Provided by publisher.
Identifiers: LCCN 2021049570 (print) | LCCN 2021049571 (ebook) | ISBN 9781771889698 (hardcover) | ISBN 9781774638729 (paperback) | ISBN 9781003127482 (ebook)
Subjects: LCSH: Internet of things--Industrial applications. | Computational intelligence--Industrial applications. | Cryptography. | Computer networks--Security measures.
Classification: LCC TK5105.8857 .A386 2022 (print) | LCC TK5105.8857 (ebook) | DDC 006.3--dc23/eng/20211102
LC record available at https://lccn.loc.gov/2021049570
LC ebook record available at https://lccn.loc.gov/2021049571

ISBN: 978-1-77188-969-8 (hbk)
ISBN: 978-1-77463-872-9 (pbk)
ISBN: 978-1-00312-748-2 (ebk)

About the Editors

Rajdeep Chowdhury, PhD (1982–2020), was an eminent academician, trend-setting author, and award-winning poet. He had more than 12 years working experience in academics. His research areas included cryptography, data warehouse, data mining, network security, etc. He authored and presented more than 90 research papers in international and national journals and conferences (ACM, Elsevier, IEEE, Springer, Scopus, Taylor & Francis, CRC Press, Thomson Reuters, Bloomsbury, Tata McGraw Hill). He also authored/edited several books and was on the editorial boards of more than 30 international journals. He also held three published patents. Dr. Chowdhury was a program committee member for more than 120 international conferences and delivered more than 30 keynote addresses and invited lectures at various international and national conferences, seminars, and symposiums all over the globe. He received many prestigious awards during his career, notably an honorary doctorate from the International Security & Strategy Studies College, Nigeria in 2019; Global Outreach Research Award 2019 for Excellence: "Outstanding Researcher in Computer Science and Engineering" at the Global Outreach Research and Education Summit & Awards 2019; 2000 Outstanding Intellectuals of the 21st Century, 9th Edition by International Biographical Centre, Cambridge, England; and many others.

Dr. Chowdhury's articles, poems, and stories have been widely anthologized in more than 60 anthologies, e–zines and periodicals, both in India and abroad. Dr. Chowdhury's authored innovative and unique book *POISINE: Bengali Cuisine with Poetry* (Level 1: Starters) is in Asia Pacific Records.

S. K. Niranjan, PhD, is Professor and Head in the Department of Computer Applications at JSS Science and Technology University (formerly Sri Jayachamarajendra College of Engineering), Mysuru, Karnataka, India. He has more than 30 years of experience in both industry and teaching. He has published more than 60 technical papers in books, journals, and conference proceedings and has been invited as general chair and technical program committee chair for many national and international conferences conducted in India and abroad, and he has also delivered keynotes at many national and international conferences.

Dr. Niranjan has been an editor for many national and international journals and conference proceedings as well. He is actively involved in many professional organizations, including IEEE, ACM, CSI, ISTE, and he has also been a member of the executive committees of the IEEE Computer Society, India Council, and the IEEE Bangalore Section. His professional interests are in image processing, pattern recognition, software engineering, business analytic, business intelligence, cloud computing, etc.

Contents

Contributors

Avhishek Adhikary
Amity School of Information Technology, Amity University Kolkata, Kolkata, India

Krishnadas Banerjee
Jemes Academy, Kolkata, West Bengal, India

Arnab Chakraborty
Amity School of Information Technology, Amity University Kolkata, Kolkata, India

Rajdeep Chowdhury
Chinsurah 712101, Hooghly, West Bengal, India

Anirban Das
Department of Computer Science, University of Engineering and Management, Kolkata, India

Anupam Das
Department of Computer Science & Engineering, Amity University, Kolkata, India

Sagar Kumar Dhawa
ICT/CS, J.C. Bose Institute of Education and Research, Bardhaman, West Bengal, India

Pushan Kumar Dutta
Amity School of Engineering and Technology, Amity University Kolkata, Kolkata, India

K. Ganaraj
Information Science & Engineering Department, Sahyadri College of Engineering and Management Adyar, Mangaluru, India

Manu Gautam
Department of Biosciences, Shri Ram College, Muzaffarnagar, Uttar Pradesh, India

Amitav Ghosh
School of Management Studies, Seacom Skills University, West Bengal, India

Megha Gupta
Department of Biotechnology, Institute of Engineering and Technology (IET), Lucknow, Uttar Pradesh, India

Madhura N. Hegde
Information Science & Engineering Department, Sahyadri College of Engineering and Management Adyar, Mangaluru, India

D. R. Janardhana
Information Science & Engineering Department, Sahyadri College of Engineering and Management Adyar, Mangaluru, India

Rita Karmakar
Amity Institute of Psychology and Allied Sciences, Amity University Kolkata, Kolkata, India

Jayapadmini Kanchan
Information Science & Engineering Department, Sahyadri College of Engineering and Management
Adyar, Mangaluru, India

Shraddha Kaushik
Department of Biotechnology, Institute of Engineering and Technology (IET), Lucknow,
Uttar Pradesh, India

K. S. Kavitha
Department of CSE, Global Academy of Technology, Bangalore, India

Smriti Kumari
Institiue of Management Studies, Banaras Hindu University, Varanasi 221005, Uttar Pradesh, India

Sukhwant Kumar
Department of Mechanical Engineering, JIS College of Engineering, Kalyani 741235, Nadia,
West Bengal, India

Paromita Mitra
KGS Technology Group, Kolkata, West Bengal, India

Saurabh Pandey
Department of Biotechnology, S. D. College of Engineering & Technology, Muzaffarnagar,
Uttar Pradesh, India

Abhipsa Pattnaik
Bachelor of Business Administration-Information Technology, Symbiosis Institute of Computer
Science and Research, Pune, India

Rishabh Pipalwa
Amity School of Information Technology, Amity University Kolkata, Kolkata, India

Rajatha
Information Science & Engineering Department, SJBIT, Bangalore, India

Mekhla Sen
Department of Electrical Engineering, Meghnad Saha Institute of Technology, Nazirabad Road,
Kolkata 700150, West Bengal, India

Sudip Siha
Seacom Skills University, West Bengal, India

Madhusudan Sharma
Bayer Crop Science Limited, Uttar Pradesh, India
Bayer Crop Science, Germany

Parshant Kumar Sharma
Department of Electrical Engineering, Kwangwoon University, Seoul, South Korea
VBRI Innovation Pvt. Ltd., New Delhi, India

Asha B. Shetty
Information Science & Engineering Department, Sahyadri College of Engineering and Management
Adyar, Mangaluru, India

Abhinav Singh
Department of Pharmaceutical Technology, NSHM Knowledge Campus, Tollygunge,
Kolkata 700053, West Bengal, India

Amarjeet Singh
Global Institute of Technology, Gurgaon, Haryana, India

Satyam Kumar Singh
Department of Civil Engineering, JIS College of Engineering, Kalyani 741235, Nadia, West Bengal, India

Sunit Kumar Singh
Department of Civil Engineering, JIS College of Engineering, Kalyani 741235, Nadia, West Bengal, India

Nishant Vats
Department Production Planning and Control; Varroc Polymers India Pvt. Ltd., Greater Noida, Uttar Pradesh, India

Abbreviations

AES	advanced encryption standard
API	application execution marker
CT	computed tomography
DES	data encryption standard
DFK	dual formula key
DKMBIET	dual key and matrix-based iterative encryption technique
DDoS	distributed denial of service
DoS	denial of service
EHRs	electronic health records
IaaS	infrastructure-as-a-service
ICT	information and communication technology
IoT	Internet of things
IPFS	interplanetary file system
LFC	logarithmic function–based cryptosystem
MRI	magnetic resonance imaging
NBFW	network based firewall
NROI	non-region of interest
PKI	public key infrastructure
PMDs	personal medical devices
RDT	rapid dissolving tablet
RFID	radio frequency identification
ROI	region of interest
SD-WAN	software define wide area network
SHC	self-healing concrete
SSCT	stochastic seed–based cryptographic technique
SSL	secure attachment layer
TRAS	trash the ash
WAN	wide area network

Preface

This new volume illustrates the diversified applications of IoT. The volume addresses the issue of data safekeeping along with the development of a new cryptographic and security technology as well as a range of other advances in IoT.

This volume, *Advances in Applications of Computational Intelligence and the Internet of Things (IoT): Cryptography and Network Security in IoT*, looks at the application of IoT in medical technology and healthcare, including the design of IoT-based mobile healthcare units and a blockchain technique based smart health record system. Other topics include a blended IoT-enabled learning approach through a study employing clustering techniques, an IoT-enabled garbage disposal system with an advanced message notification system through an android application, IoT-based self-healing concrete that uses bacteria and environmental waste, an IoT-enabled trash-the-ash application that regulates flow, and more.

The fresh and innovative advances that demonstrate computational intelligence and IoT in practice that are discussed in this volume will be informative for academicians, scholars, scientists, industry professionals, policymakers, government and nongovernment organizations, and others.

We hope that the chapters will inspire prospective researchers, particularly those who are interested and involved in interdisciplinary research, in their work. The content of the book should be of keen interest to academicians, industrial experts, researchers, and practitioners from diverse disciplines.

We hope that the book will provide a platform for academicians, scholars, scientists, industrial professionals, policymakers, and government and non-government organizations to share new and innovative advances in theory, analytical approaches, numerical simulations, demon-strations, case studies, laboratory results, operational tests, and ongoing expansions with significant advancements in the field of computational intelligence and the internet of things.

CHAPTER 1

A New Cryptographic Modus Operandi Approach Based on Amalgamation of Physics and Chemistry

SUKHWANT KUMAR[1*], SMRITI KUMARI[2], and
RAJDEEP CHOWDHURY[3]

[1]*Department of Mechanical Engineering, JIS College of Engineering, Kalyani 741235, Nadia, West Bengal, India*

[2]*Institiue of Management Studies, Banaras Hindu University, Varanasi 221005, Uttar Pradesh, India*

[3]*Chinsurah 712101, Hooghly, West Bengal, India*

Corresponding author. E-mail: 00saket08@gmail.com

ABSTRACT

Nowadays technology is everywhere. The impact of technology in modern times is immeasurable. At the present time, we cannot imagine our life without technology. We are living in an environment surrounded by technologies. As every coin has two sides, the same goes with technology. It has negative as well as positive aspects. There are many ways to share our data, but most of our data is being stolen or viewed by others without our knowledge. Persistent digital offenders, disappointed present and previous allies, and indiscreet clients can compromise our computer systems and bargain information. Security of the equipment, programs, arrangements, and strategies is intended to protect against both inside and outer dangers to our organization's network and computer frameworks. Different layers of equipment and programs can keep an eye on harmful systems and prevent them from spreading on the off chance that they might slip past our safeguards. So, in order to save our data, cryptography is being used. Cipher texting is a modern-day technology-based application that is known as encrypted or encoded information. It is usually performed on a plain text using an algorithm. The algorithm is basically known as cipher. In modern times, there are many modus operandi for cryptography, but we have developed a new modus operandi of cryptography that is mainly designed for better security. It is a very simple and convenient two-tier system as we have used the simple or basic concepts of physics and chemistry.

1.1   INTRODUCTION

Due to the advancement of technology, cybercrimes are increasing at an alarming rate. In order to overcome this situation, cryptography has acted as a boon. Cryptography is the study of techniques for securing data in the form of encryption performed on plain text using an algorithm. Cipher texting is the outcome of encryption, so it is also known as encrypted or encoded data. This chapter presents an approach of securing data through cipher texting. It includes a way of amalgamation of theories of different disciples such as physics and chemistry. The De Broglie hypothesis and law of motion have given a solution that has acted as our cipher text. The process includes encryption and decryption of an ASCII value (Table 1.1) that can be converted to original text. The information however cannot be viewed without decrypting it, so the overall process goes in a cyclic manner. This work involves creating, writing, or generating codes with an aim to keep data secured. It provides a security to our data and authentication to our communication.

1.2   LITERATURE REVIEW

1.2.1   MATRIX AND MUTATION-BASED CRYPTOSYSTEM

It is the foremost type of cryptographic modus operandi, which is based on matrix and mutation. It mainly deals with shifting of rows and columns with the hexadecimal system. The color code is used in order to obtain the cipher text. The algorithm is usually compared with GFC and TDES. It is mainly based on text files (.txt), executable files (.exe), and dynamic link libraries (.dll). Both encryption and decryption methods have been proposed in this chapter.

The consequences show that matrix and mutation–based cryptosystem (MMC) takes less time for encryption and also decryption than TDES and also takes less or same time than GFC. Also, it is a fact that homogeneity is maintained by the consequences.

1.2.2   DUAL KEY AND MATRIX–BASED ITERATIVE ENCRYPTION TECHNIQUE (DKMBIET)

This work is basically related to transferring the data safely. In order to assure safe transfer of data, a dual key is generated. At first, a key is generated according to the number of characters in the key text, and then another key is engendered for employing the key. The employment of another key is done in the encryption process so that a 16-bit key is engendered. The dual-key engendering helps in making the algorithm stronger for keeping the data safe.

1.2.3   LOGARITHMIC FUNCTION–BASED CRYPTOSYSTEM (LFC)

The main purpose of this work is to minimize the complexity of time. A symmetric key modus operandi is employed to achieve it. The key used at the time of encryption and decryption is used in logarithmic function–based cryptosystem (LFC). The endangering of three generations of numbers usually makes the security key much stronger. The key of modus operandi is made by taking the highest and lowest from the three generations. Genetic functions such as crossover and mutation are also added during the formulation of algorithm. The files used for testing the algorithm are the text files and DLL files, whereas the consequences demonstrate that the LFC is in vicinity in all respects with RSA and TDES.

1.2.4   STOCHASTIC SEED–BASED CRYPTOGRAPHIC TECHNIQUE (SSCT) USING DUAL FORMULA KEY (DFK)

This algorithm is also symmetric key cryptographic modus operandi, which is the same as the previous algorithm. It usually makes the algorithm fast, although in this algorithm, unlike in symmetric key cryptography, the key is usually not sent through any secure medium to the receiver. It could be hacked by the hackers as the medium through which it is being shared is not protected enough. The key is merged with the cipher text instead of sending the key separately. The transmission is being secured, and hence it is protected from the upcoming risk as it becomes difficult for the hackers to hack it. In this algorithm, the final key is crafted by merging the two engendered keys. The attribute of the algorithm is that for a piece character, a 256-digit binary number would be engendered, which eventually helps in keeping the cipher text safe.

1.2.5   DESIGN AND IMPLEMENTATION OF RNS MODEL–BASED STEGANOGRAPHY TECHNIQUE FOR SECURED TRANSMISSION

The modus operandi in this chapter is based on steganography while the data is hidden within the image. The model that is proposed in the algorithm is RNS while the RNS object includes the formation of the front as well as the back image. The alpha factor is employed for the combination of both the images. The combination of both the images depends upon the value of alpha factor. If the alpha factor is 0.5 then both the images are combined equally. If the value of the alpha factor is less than 0.5 then the image at the back is more than the image at the front.

The image however obtained is a stego image that gives an impression to the viewers about the coordinates only and does not give a direction. This is the reason due to which the security parameter of the proposed modus operandi is augmented or sharpened.

1.3   PROPOSED WORK

In this section, we will discuss our work in a descriptive manner along with illustrations, comparative chart, graphs, and flowchart diagrams (Fig. 1.1).

1.3.1   ENCRYPTION

Here $g = 9.8$ m/s^2, $h = 6.67 \times 10^{-34}$, $m = 9.1 \times 10^{-31}$. This value would remain constant throughout.

Take an example of a ball that needs to be launched vertically upwards. So, we throw this ball vertically upwards against gravity. While going upwards, its velocity will begin to decrease, and after reaching a certain height, imagine that suddenly gravitational force becomes zero. Now this ball begins to move with a constant velocity V. Since the ball is moving with a constant velocity, the constituent electron would also have the same velocity. Let us switch to microscopic point of view and consider a single electron moving with a velocity; this would satisfy de Broglie's hypothesis, that is,

$$\lambda \text{ (lambda)} = h/m \times V.$$

and emit a wave of wavelength lambda.

Now consider these ASCII values to be your initial velocity of the ball, and position of these characters Table 1.2 to be analogous to time and ($g = 9.8$) is kept constant (g = acceleration due to gravity). Final velocity at a certain height is calculated to be

$$V = (U - g \times p).$$

This time the ball is going vertically upward. Hence, we have applied the equation for motion under gravity for vertically upward motion, that is,

$$V = (U - g \times p).$$

After attaining this velocity, the ball moves out of the gravitational field of earth and begins to move with a fixed velocity V (just now calculated). Now the wavelength emitted by the electron wave is calculated as lambda using De Broglie hypothesis. This wavelength is our cipher text (Table 1.3).

Let us consider a plain text, that is, @12Saket.

Step 1 Get the ASCII code for the plain text (Table 1.4).

TABLE 1.1   Evaluation of Text to ASCII Value.

@	1	2	S	a	K	E	t
64	49	50	83	97	107	101	116

Step 2 Using equation of motion under gravity. Where g is constant.

TABLE 1.2 Calculation Chart.

Position	U (initial velocity)	U + (g × p)	V = U + (g × p)
1	64	64 + (9.8 × 1)	73.8
2	49	49 + (9.8 × 2)	68.6
3	50	50 + (9.8 × 3)	79.4
4	83	83 + (9.8 × 4)	122.2
5	97	97 + (9.8 × 5)	146
6	107	107 + (9.8 × 6)	165.8
7	101	101 + (9.8 × 7)	169.6
8	116	116 + (9.8 × 8)	194.4

Step 3 Considering that the ball is made of electron having velocity the same as ball using De Broglie wave equation, that is,

$$\lambda = \frac{h}{mV},$$

where lambda is wavelength, h is Plank's constant, m is the mass of electron, V is the velocity of electron (Table 1.3); $h = 6.63 \times 10^{-34}$, the mass of electron 9.1×10^{-31}.

TABLE 1.3 Continuation of Table 1.2.

V (velocity of electron)	h/mV	Cipher text (λ)
73.8	$0.72 \times 10^{-3} \times 73.8$	0.053136
68.6	$0.72 \times 10^{-3} \times 68.6$	0.049352
79.4	$0.72 \times 10^{-3} \times 79.4$	0.057168
122.2	$0.72 \times 10^{-3} \times 122.2$	0.087984
136.2	$0.72 \times 10^{-3} \times 146$	0.10512
156	$0.72 \times 10^{-3} \times 165.8$	0.119376
159.8	$0.72 \times 10^{-3} \times 169.6$	0.122112
184.6	$0.72 \times 10^{-3} \times 194.4$	0.139968

TABLE 1.4 Evaluated Table of Encryption Process.

Plain text	Cipher text
@	0.053136
1	0.049352
2	0.057168

TABLE 1.4 *(Continued)*

Plain text	Cipher text
S	0.087984
A	0.10512
K	0.119376
E	0.122112
T	0.139968

1.3.2 DECRYPTION

Here also $g = 9.8$

Now the cipher text is your wavelength (lambda). Just follow the reverse procedure of encryption.

Imagine the electron to be at that point where the gravitational forces turn out to be zero (Table 1.5).

$$V = h/m \times \text{lambda}.$$

Till now we were judging the phenomena from a microscopic point of view. Let us switch back to the macroscopic point of view. Consider the ball as a whole. The ball is about to enter the earth's gravitational field, thereby validating the equations of motion under gravity, for downward fall. Now the final velocity that was attained at this point is considered as the initial velocity (Table 1.6).

Hence, we get back ASCII codes (Fig. 1.2),

$$U = V + g \times p.$$

This ball (your message) begins to fall under gravity and finally reaches the receiver with a velocity (i.e., ASCII values). Now again we get ASCII values that can be easily converted back to original text. This time the ball is going downwards. Hence, we have applied the equation for motion under gravity for vertically downward motion, that is,

$$U = V + g \times p.$$

This equation is familiar to us as we have already dealt with this equation in school.

Step 1 Take the cipher text and divide by 0.72×10^{-3}

TABLE 1.5   Decryption Process.

Cipher text/(h/m) λ	V (velocity of electron)
0.053136/0.72 × 10⁻³	73.8
0.049352/0.72 × 10⁻³	68.6
0.057168/0.72 × 10⁻³	79.4
0.087984/0.72 × 10⁻³	122.2
0.10512/0.72 × 10⁻³	146
0.119376/0.72 × 10⁻³	165.8
0.122112/0.72 × 10⁻³	169.6
0.139968/0.72 × 10⁻³	194.4

Step 2 By V we can calculate U, that is, ASCII value of our plain text.

TABLE 1.6   Decryption Process Continuation of Table 1.5.

$U = V - g \times p$	Position	$V - g \times p$	U (initial velocity)
73.8	1	73.8 − (9.8 × 1)	64
68.6	2	68.6 − (9.8 × 2)	49
79.4	3	79.4 − (9.8 × 3)	50
122.2	4	122.2 − (9.8 × 4)	83
146	5	146 − (9.8 × 5)	97
165.8	6	165.8 − (9.8 × 6)	107
169.6	7	169.6 − (9.8 × 7)	101
194.4	8	194.4 − (9.8 × 8)	116

Step 3 Now convert ASCII value in to plain text (Table 1.7).

TABLE 1.7   Evaluated Table of Decryption Process.

64	49	50	83	97	107	101	116
↓	↓	↓	↓	↓	↓	↓	↓
@	1	2	S	a	K	e	T

In this entire algorithm, dissipative effects are ignored. Hence, we have simply applied the equation for motion under gravity. And after reaching a certain height, the gravitational field is imagined to be zero and switching from macroscopic to microscopic point of view. The process is reversed in case of decryption.

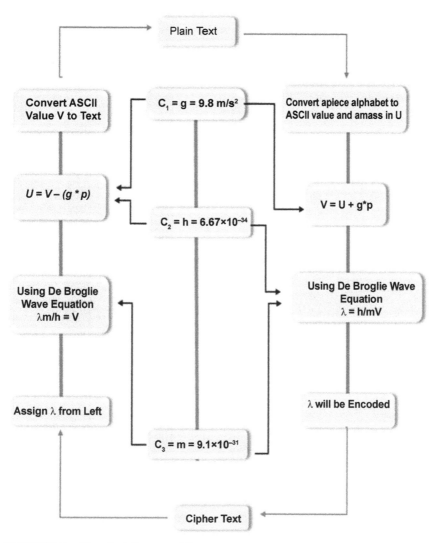

FIGURE 1.1 Flowchart diagram of the process.

Dec	Hex	Name	Char	Ctrl-char	Dec	Hex	Char	Dec	Hex	Char	Dec	Hex	Char
0	0	Null	NUL	CTRL-@	32	20	Space	64	40	@	96	60	
1	1	Start of heading	SCH	CTRL-A	33	21	!	65	41	A	97	61	a
2	2	Start of text	STX	CTRL-B	34	22	"	66	42	B	98	62	b
3	3	End of text	ETX	CTRL-C	35	23	#	67	43	C	99	63	c
4	4	End to xmit	EOT	CTRL-D	36	24	$	68	44	D	100	64	d
5	5	Enquiry	ENQ	CTRL-E	37	25	%	69	45	E	101	65	e
6	6	Acknowledge	ACK	CTRL-F	38	26	&	70	46	F	102	66	f
7	7	Bell	BEL	CTRL-G	39	27	'	71	47	G	103	67	g
8	8	Back space	BS	CTRL-H	40	28	(	72	48	H	104	68	h
9	9	Horizontal tab	HT	CTRL-I	41	29	)	73	49	I	105	69	i
10	0A	Line feed	LF	CTRL-J	42	2A	*	74	4A	J	106	6A	j
11	0B	Vertical tab	VT	CTRL-K	43	2B	+	75	4B	K	107	6B	k
12	0C	Form feed	FF	CTRL-L	44	2C	,	76	4C	L	108	6C	l
13	0D	Carriage feed	CR	CTRL-M	45	2D	-	77	4D	M	109	6D	m
14	0E	Shift out	SO	CTRL-N	46	2E	.	78	4E	N	110	6E	n
15	0F	Shift in	SI	CTRL-O	47	2F	/	79	4F	O	111	6F	o
16	10	Data line escape	DLE	CTRL-P	48	30	0	80	50	P	112	70	p
17	11	Device control 1	DC1	CTRL-Q	49	31	1	81	51	Q	113	71	q
18	12	Device control 2	DC2	CTRL-R	50	32	2	82	52	R	114	72	r
19	13	Device control 3	DC3	CTRL-S	51	33	3	83	53	S	115	73	s
20	14	Device control 4	DC4	CTRL-T	52	34	4	84	54	T	116	74	t
21	15	Neg acknowledge	NAK	CTRL-U	53	35	5	85	55	U	117	75	u
22	16	Synchronous idle	SYN	CTRL-V	54	36	6	86	56	V	118	76	v
23	17	End of xmit block	ETB	CTRL-W	55	37	7	87	57	W	119	77	w
24	18	Cancel	CAN	CTRL-X	56	38	8	88	58	X	120	78	x
25	19	End of medium	EM	CTRL-Y	57	39	9	89	59	Y	121	79	y
26	1A	Substitute	SUB	CTRL-Z	58	3A	:	90	5A	Z	122	7A	z
27	1B	Escape	ESC	CTRL-[	59	3B	;	91	5B	[	123	7B	{
28	1C	File separator	FS	CTRL-/	60	3C	<	92	5C	\	124	7C		
29	1D	Group separator	GS	CTRL-]	61	3D	=	93	5D	]	125	7D	}
30	1E	Record separator	RS	CTRL-^	62	3E	>	94	5E	^	126	7E	~
31	1F	Unit separator	US	CTRL-_	63	3F	?	95	5F	_	127	7F	DEL

FIGURE 1.2   ASCII value table.

1.4   RESULT ANALYSIS

This section deals with the comparison and analysis of our proposed work and gives a possible summary of our work (Figs. 1.3–1.6). Here we have compared our work with AES and TDES. Comparison is done on the parameter of encryption and decryption time-lapse during compiling three different files, dynamic link libraries (.dll), text (.txt), and document files (.doc) (Tables 1.8–1.10).

TABLE 1.8 For .dll Files.

Sl. no.	Source file name	Source file size (in bytes)	CMPC (in m/s)		AES (in m/s)		TDES (in m/s)	
			Enc.	Dec.	Enc.	Dec.	Enc.	Dec.
1	File1.dll	3004	13	0	17	0	8	9
2	File2.dll	6547	15	15	0	0	18	0
3	File3.dll	11,241	14	16	17	13	19	21
4	File4.dll	26,147	32	32	4	0	33	30
5	File5.dll	45,014	32	33	0	32	35	21
6	File6.dll	90,114	34	34	3	32	34	25
7	File7.dll	254,712	33	35	1	16	43	33
8	File8.dll	345,895	55	58	11	31	71	77
9	File9.dll	492,147	62	60	33	43	215	234
10	File10.dll	914,498	139	142	30	64	184	186
11	File11.dll	1247,896	205	213	79	125	264	458
12	File12.dll	2,001,478	277	287	46	98	394	509
13	File13.dll	2,498,771	413	408	74	125	535	517
14	File14.dll	3,326,788	486	490	101	174	816	753
15	File15.dll	3,589,953	558	578	101	176	896	927
16	File16.dll	4,347,926	644	662	124	208	907	899
17	File17.dll	4,412,682	695	671	140	269	928	961
18	File18.dll	4,774,179	788	781	144	211	967	1033
19	File19.dll	5,256,511	789	796	144	213	1189	1175
20	File20.dll	5,547,891	800	813	147	255	1172	1149

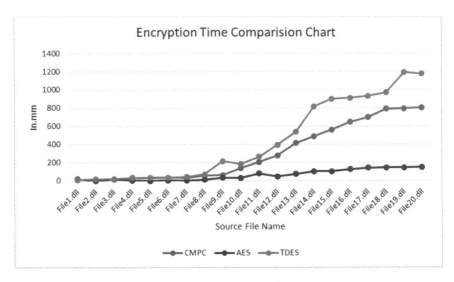

FIGURE 1.3   Decryption time comparison chart for .dll file.

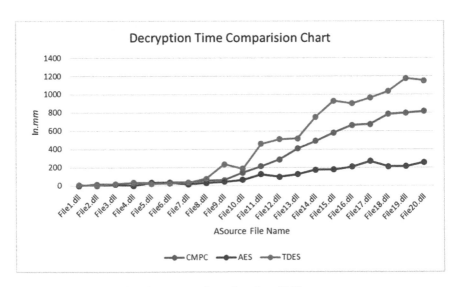

FIGURE 1.4   Encryption time comparison chart for .dll file.

TABLE 1.9   For .doc Files.

Sl. no.	Source file name	Source file size (in bytes)	CMPC (in m/s)		AES (in m/s)		TDES (in m/s)	
			Enc.	Dec.	Enc.	Dec.	Enc.	Dec.
1	File1.doc	35,065	16	02	0	31	16	16
2	File2.doc	39,535	17	15	16	15	16	0
3	File3.doc	50,688	30	10	16	15	16	16
4	File4.doc	63,193	16	33	16	16	15	16
5	File5.doc	126,660	32	33	16	16	32	31
6	File6.doc	351,333	16	30	16	31	109	78
7	File7.doc	555,356	33	31	16	46	125	110
8	File8.doc	659,568	71	77	31	47	141	156
9	File9.doc	1,130,596	198	123	32	62	234	329
10	File10.doc	1,595,905	231	262	63	99	562	329
11	File11.doc	3,019,338	306	317	63	94	409	421
12	File12.doc	3,386,105	321	344	125	199	692	494
13	File13.doc	3,635,353	431	511	99	125	692	562
14	File14.doc	3,053,850	455	466	99	125	912	656
15	File15.doc	3,356,556	494	491	192	140	965	960
16	File16.doc	3,655,668	558	592	109	192	950	922
17	File17.doc	5,066,056	615	562	125	192	1000	944
18	File18.doc	5,563,856	700	694	125	203	990	939
19	File19.doc	5,655,556	956	937	141	203	1031	1395
20	File20.doc	5,356,605	995	931	266	219	1046	1125

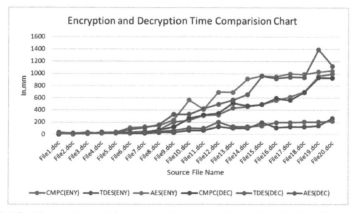

FIGURE 1.5   Encryption and decryption time comparison chart for .doc file.

TABLE 1.10   For .txt. Files.

Sl. no.	Source file name	Source file size (in bytes)	CMPC 1 (in m. sec.)		AES (in m. sec.)		TDES (in m. sec.)	
			Enc.	Dec.	Enc.	Dec.	Enc.	Dec.
1	File1.txt	2565	14	15	16	0	0	16
2	File2.txt	8282	16	3	62	0	0	16
3	File3.txt	26,585	32	13	328	0	16	0
4	File4.txt	52,852	36	33	36	13	16	0
5	File5.txt	82,825	60	31	333	13	13	16
6	File6.txt	157,848	31	30	31	32	31	31
7	File7.txt	343,587	107	70	47	32	125	141
8	File8.txt	737,157	144	95	62	48	250	152
9	File9.txt	782,732	153	157	89	63	159	215
10	File10.txt	1,375,453	213	158	89	89	291	329
11	File11.txt	1,737,050	254	297	94	94	344	360
12	File12.txt	2,107,551	327	358	109	125	438	453
13	File13.txt	2,770,747	502	462	158	235	562	641
14	File14.txt	3,284,377	521	538	140	156	815	865
15	File15.txt	3,785,411	611	586	298	313	953	1109
16	File16.txt	4,477,700	814	694	152	203	1210	953
17	File17.txt	5,023,407	927	892	265	215	1210	1125
18	File18.txt	5,478,827	932	981	203	250	1359	1156
19	File19.txt	5,773,500	927	965	215	329	1215	1266
20	File20.txt	7,577,277	989	1214	215	359	1422	1512

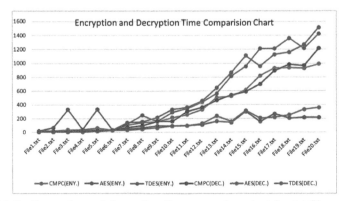

FIGURE 1.6   Encryption and decryption time comparison chart for .txt file.

1.5 CONCLUSION

By a comprehensive analysis of existing papers based on modus operandi of cryptography that are used currently, we came to an understanding that a continuous modification or new approach should be made for security purpose based on cryptography. The abovementioned approach is a micro-cum-macro-based formulation of physics and chemistry with two-tier security encryption and decryption system, and this work can help or progress the vivid area of methods that are still not excelled; along with that, it will work as a reference for future researchers as it contains a comparative and analytical analysis.

KEYWORDS

- **cryptographic algorithm**
- **chemistry**
- **physics**
- **lambda**
- **electron**
- **velocity**

REFERENCES

Chowdhury, R.; Bose, R.; Sengupta, N.; De, M. In *Logarithmic Formula Generated Seed Based Cryptographic Technique Using Proposed Alphanumeric Number System and Rubik Rotation Algorithm*, IEEE 2012 International Conference on Communications, Devices and Intelligent Systems (CODIS 2012), Published and Archived in IEEE Digital Explore, 2012; pp 564–567; ISBN–978-1-4673-4700-6.

Chowdhury, R.; Chatterjee, P.; Mitra, P.; Roy, O. Design and Implementation of Security Mechanism for Data Warehouse Performance Enhancement Using Two Tier User Authentication Techniques. *Int. J. Innov. Res. Sci. Eng. Technol.* **2014,** *3* (6), 165–172; ISSN (Print)–2347 6710, ISSN (Online)–2319 8753.

Chowdhury, R.; Dey, N.; Ghosh, S. Design and Implementation of RNS Model Based Steganographic Technique for Secured Transmission. *Int. J. Adv. Res. Comput. Sci. Softw. Eng.* **2012,** *2* (3), 132–136; ISSN–2277 6451 (P), ISSN–2277 128X (O).

Chowdhury, R.; Dutta, S.; De, M. Towards Design, Analysis and Performance Enhancement of Data Warehouse by Implementation and Simulation of P2P Technology on Proposed

Pseudo Mesh Architecture. *Int. J. Innov. Res. Sci. Eng. Technol.* **2014,** *3* (6), 178–187; ISSN (Print)–2347 6710, ISSN (Online)–2319 8753.

Chowdhury, R.; Gupta, S.; Saha, A. In *Stochastic Seed Based Cryptographic Technique [SSCT] Using Dual Formula Key [DFK]*, Proceedings of International Conference on Communication and Industrial Applications, ICCIA 2011, Published and Archived in IEEE Digital Xplore, 2011; pp 1–5; ISBN–978-1-4577-1915-8.

Chowdhury, R.; Mitra, P.; Ghosh, R.; Kumar, S. Data Warehouse Safekeeping Augmentation Employing Cryptographic Modus Operandi: Comprehensive Study and Comparative Analysis. *Int. J. Emerg. Trends Technol. Comput. Sci. (IJETTCS)* **2017,** *6* (6), 062–068; ISSN 2278-6856.

Chowdhury, R.; Pal, B. Proposed Hybrid Data Warehouse Architecture Based on Data Model. *Int. J. Comput. Sci. Commun.* **2010,** *1* (2), 211–213; ISSN–0973 7391, UGC Approved Journal with Serial Number–48710.

Chowdhury, R.; Pal, B.; De, M. Proposed Business Principles Governing Enterprise Data Warehouse Design: Conceptual Framework with Enhancement of Knowledge Infrastructure via Context Model. *Res. J. Sci. Technol.* **2011,** *3* (4), 212–216; ISSN (Print)–0975 4393, ISSN (Online)–2349 2988, UGC Approved Journal with Serial Number–49210.

Chowdhury, R.; Pal, B.; Ghosh, A.; De, M. In *A Data Warehouse Architectural Design Using Proposed Pseudo Mesh Schema*, First International Conference on Intelligent Infrastructure, CSI ICII 2012, 47th Annual National Convention of Computer Society of India, Tata McGraw Hill Education Private Limited, 2012; pp 138–141; ISBN (13)–978-1-25-906170-7, ISBN (10)–978-1-25-906170-1.

Chowdhury, R.; Saha, A.; Biswas, P. In *Dual Key and Matrix Based Iterative Encryption Technique [DKMBIET]*, Proceedings of International Conference on Convergence of Optics and Electronics, COE 2011, Science City, Kolkata, 2011; pp 75–84; ISBN–978-8-1906-4011-4.

Chowdhury, R.; Saha, A.; Biswas, P.; Dutta, A. Matrix and Mutation Based Cryptosystem [MMC]. *Int. J. Comput. Sci. Netw. Secur.* **2011,** *11* (3), 7–14; ISSN–1738 7906, Indexed in Thomson Reuters Master Journal List.

Chowdhury, R.; Saha, A.; Dutta, A. Logarithmic Function Based Cryptosystem [LFC]. *Int. J. Comput. Inf. Syst.* **2011,** *2* (4), 70–76; ISSN–2229 5208, Indexed in Thomson Reuters Master Journal List.

Pal, B.; Chattopadhyay, S.; Mitra, S.; Chowdhury, R.; De, M. Study and Comparison of Indexing Models in Data Warehouse. *Int. J. Softw. Eng. Res. Practices* **2012,** *2* (3), 1–8; ISSN (Print)–2231 2048, ISSN (Online)–2231 0320.

Santos, R. J.; Bernardino, J.; Vieira, M. In *A Survey on Data Security in Data Warehousing: Issues, Challenges and Opportunities*, International Conference on Computer as a Tool; EUROCON IEEE, Lisbon, 2011; pp 1–4; INSPEC Accession Number–12075581, Published and Archived in IEEE Digital Xplore; ISBN–978-1-4244-7486-8.

Saurabh, A. K.; Nagpal, B. A Survey on Current Security Strategies in Data Warehouses. *Int. J. Eng. Sci. Technol.* **2011,** *3* (4), pp 3484–3488; ISSN–0975 5462.

Vieira, M.; Vieira, J.; Madeira, H. In *Towards Data Security in Affordable Data Warehouse*, 7th European Dependable Computing Conference.

CHAPTER 2

Application of Cryptography and Network Security in the Internet of Things (IoT)

K. S. KAVITHA*

Department of CSE, Global Academy of Technology, Bangalore, India

*E-mail: drkavitha2015@gmail.com

ABSTRACT

This chapter discusses the importance of cybersecurity, its origin, and various aspects. Basic concepts related to cryptography are given for the reader to understand the importance of cryptography for cybersecurity, and then the concept of the cybersecurity and network security is also explained and clarified the meaning of both. The discussion ends with recent technological developments of cybersecurity.

The future of this technology is considered as Internet of things (IoT). The IoT basics, working of IoT devices, applications of IoT for various fields, and problems associated with IoT are explained with simple examples.

Whatever the process and processing devices they are facing cyberattacks and hacking, so this chapter explains the concept of various security options and measures along with drawbacks of each type of security system and then discusses in length about the weakness of the security where the possible threats exist. The IoT security aspects and related issues are explained in detail.

The chapter ends with the latest and future cybersecurity trends and issues along with the IoT and future possible developments in the field of cybersecurity and IoT technologies.

2.1 OBJECTIVE OF THE CHAPTER

The reader will generally get the basic knowledge about concept of cyber-security, cryptography, Internet of thing (IoT), and the future of all these technologies along with the relationship between these. Also, the reader will know that future of technology is cybersecurity and IoT.

2.1.1 CYBERSECURITY

Cybersecurity also called IT security or information technology security or simply computer security is a system of processes and technologies developed to safeguard the networks, programs, data, and devices against any attacks or unauthorized accessing or causing damage.

Cybersecurity includes network security, application security, data security, database security, Infrastructure security, mobile security, cloud security, etc.

Network security is a process of protection for the access to files and directories in the computer network against any unauthorized access, misuse, hacking, modification, destruction, malfunction, etc. so that it provides a highly secured platform and environment for the computer users.

The main objective of implementation of cybersecurity is to protect the integrity of data and provisions to be implemented defense system against any threats and attacks. In this context, Beach, Logan et al. analyze the 18 design principles presented in the National Institute of Standards and Technology Special Publication 800–160 Volume 1 and verified its usefulness in developing secure and resilient systems by understanding how these design principles can consistently and effectively be employed to meet security and resiliency requirements.[1]

Similarly, we are also aware that another major security threat is DDoS attack, which really becomes problem when IoT devices are controlled using computers and especially in wireless network systems that target the victim system and prevent the legitimate user for accessing the network resources and services; an approach by Aldaej is based on the analysis of bandwidth attacks focusing on DDoS and studied how the performance of the network decreases.[2]

After introducing Wi-Fi and Bluetooth features, the computers are more vulnerable to various known and unknown attacks that regularly made the researchers to innovate new technologies and futuristic methods to avoid attacks and hacking of hardware and software systems. Presently, another type of cybercriminal attacks are in increase called online identity theft, online cheating, online fraud, and financial frauds, which have to be considered seriously. For example, ransomware attack even though looks simple but the effect of this attack creates serious problems. Suppose, when the user opens unknown e-mails or uses/downloads software from unknown and untrusted entity, the ransomware software enters into the system and the attacker sitting in an undisclosed place sees all the information and locks all the possible login options, then he sends messages through e-mail or through other means and demands for some ransom—it may vary from mere thousands to crores depending on the person and the importance of information/data kept in the computer /laptop—if you do not pay the ransom, there is 100% chance, they will erase all the information and damage the whole system; or if they find personal and confidential information, there is a risk of leaking such information, video, or data such as photos and videos to all social networking sites and all the persons through e-mail accounts that are in the user's contact list and damaging to the reputation of the person. Virus attack on the virtual systems and virtual environment is also a serious concern. As the demand for more data, and faster download also, increased the cyberattacks and cybercrimes, in this situation, the aspect of cybersecurity has got wider effect on the activities of the world.

The issues of cybersecurity are taken a new dimension with the introduction of cyber-physical systems, wherein the integration happens between computer systems, networking, physical processes, and the complete I/O devices that offer closed control and monitoring of the process virtually also. It blends users with computers in such a way that all machines, computer, and software are united in a systemic way which we can see in various situations, including semiautonomous vehicles to wearable devices. But this creates serious problems as it lacks advanced security systems in place—once the security is breached, defiantly havoc will happen. As the cyber-physical systems also include robots, drones, all related security issues cannot be implemented in one software, as various systems require their own type of security systems and platforms. When these are all integrated the conflict between these, security issues will arise, so robust security system that integrates all the needs of security issues of all these integrated devices is very important.

Lai, Qiu et al. propose a realistic model to investigate the cascading failure process in a cyber-physical power system that can be topologically modeled as an interdependent system with power network and a cyber-network.[3] This analysis helps us to think the development of robust security systems for IoT devices in near future.

As IoT devices are also involved in cyber-physical systems, the complexity of cybersecurity issues will further increase and create a herculean problem of implementing robust security platform for all these different systems, wherein IoT are quite simple in construction and operation. Whereas the robots are complex in both construction and operation, artificial intelligence creates a sea change in the use of electronic and computer devices as these are beginning to think logically, which again creates problem toward security and any attack on these systems. The robots or IoT devices will do the opposite things which they are not meant for and also they are acting as slaves under the control of hackers and pass on very confidential information to the hacker; many times these systems are hacked in such a way that the genuine users do not come to know about the hacking.

2.1.2   INTERNET OF THINGS (IOT)

Various processes are controlled by devices through Internet is called IoT. Even though it is not new, for many years, it is at the initial stage of development as the Internet slowly entered into the digital controlling of day-to-day equipment and instruments, for example, many years back, the refrigerator was just a cooling instrument, but now it includes various features and fully digitized, neural network, and artificial intelligence is incorporated so that now refrigerators can also think. A house or a street or the whole city can be controlled by the various mechanisms and systems such as street lighting traffic control, drainage system—because of IoT. It is also entered into agriculture, medicine, and other process industries, entertainment industry, etc.

As IoT devices were machine-to-machine type initially, now and in future, it is so much interfaced that machine–human–machine type, because of biosensors and DevOps along with AI- and neural network–related developments, contributes high-level IoT systems. To understand these developments, we should understand various threats and its mechanisms, intrusion techniques, and prevention. It is best discussed by Abomhara and Køien, where they exhaustively gave various aspects of threats, intrusion, and prevention techniques.[4]

Similarly, Siboni, Sachidananda et al. propose an innovative security test bed framework targeted at IoT devices. It is aimed at performing advanced security testing for all types of IoT devices, with various configurations of both software and hardware using IoT scenarios, and this is based on machine learning algorithms to monitor the overall operation of the IoT device under test. This is widely helpful to check and take decision on the vulnerabilities of security flaws of IoT devices.[5]

Musaddiq, Zikaria et al. discussed on IoT devices, and its OS resource management mechanisms such as Contiki, Tiny OS, and FreeRTOS, are investigated.[6] This discussion really helped in larger way to understand the OS resource management in IoT system and to look upon the implementation of advanced and smaller size security software so that IoT devices are self-reliable and potent against any attacks.

As we are aware that IoT installation and usage in urban areas are more complex, Wi-Fi networks, mobile networks, etc. are all used at various levels of IoT usage that gives rise to problems to IoT device security issues that clearly are analyzed by Hassan and Awad, where they proposed to identify the potential prospects and privacy challenges emerged from IoT deployment in urban environments and reviewed the various aspects of security and privacy issues for IoT implementation at the residential, office, industry, regional, and city areas.[7]

IoT offers extension of remote connectivity between physical devices through Internet, causes drastic changes in our daily life, and offers more secured, low-wastage, high-performance, good-quality, long-lasting system and mechanism that can be trusted.

IoT is the outcome of a combination of various technologies such as sensor technology robotics, AI, wireless networks, embedded systems, machine learning, and automation and control.

IoT has got applications in various fields that include medical and health-care transportation, consumer electronics, smart city, smart home and smart village, building and home automation, manufacturing and process industries, agriculture, sericulture, fisheries, horticulture, energy and power management, water management, environmental management, to name few.

Generally, an IoT system consists of three parts, devices (sensors and actuators), gateway (data preprocessing units, secured cloud connectivity, etc.), and cloud (secured Internet environment with microservice architecture).

IoT devices even though looks like independent device system, but practically, it is not; individually, no device offers the fullest automation provided the area of application and place where we are using it. The computer system with IoT systems is not advanced, the microcontrollers working with low memory cannot hold large software, so implementing security software within the IoT devices is not possible because of the following reason: presently existing software requires more memory space and each works for related applications, so developing exclusively advanced and highly potent security software with possibility of requiring low memory space is the main constraint, so attacks on the IoT devices are inevitable. Attacking on the IoT devices makes things worse and causes large damage to the installation and life of people. If the attack on IoT devices that are used in advanced processing industries, refineries, high-rise buildings, and other processing industries creates serious issues of functioning of these organizations, frankly speaking, drones are also a type of IoT device that can also be controlled through Internet and remote console. Managing the IoT devices against cyberattacks is really big task, in present-day situation, we cannot predict what are the weak points of IoT devices. The sensors are considered as weak point of any IoT devices, if the sensors are hacked and wrong information were fed, nobody can imagine the havoc created by IoT devices. We also know that IoT devices are controlled or operated by using password mechanisms, here also various types of passwords are in use—it may be using letters with numbers/alphabets/special characters, using biometric passwords like fingerprint/eye retina information/voice/image identification; also these are can be hackled or modified or even the database of the parameters can be altered physically or remotely and it causes extensive damages to the system and life of the people who are using or nearby. For example, if the whole IoT system is hacked at the home, all the controls of IoT locking, entertainment, control systems are under control of hacker, and then he can do anything on the IoT systems of that house, which is really dangerous if the same is expanded to certain area or city or at the state or national level.

Few IoT devices having advanced password or operating mechanisms like voice identification and or image identification will create havoc in some cases such as if the user/house owner got throat infection/operation, no IoT devices cannot listen to him or recognition of voice commands.

As the world rapidly moves in the direction of using IoT systems, in almost all areas, the demand for using IoT devices is geometrically increasing as per estimates that the number of IoT devices exceeds 200 million in 2020. The future is bright for IoT industry; at present, the security of IoT is still a question as a number of devices and users are handling security aspects of these devices and systems are also in great demand, the problems of hacking and identity theft, sabotage, etc. may be matter of concern about IoT devices. High-level cryptographic software and hardware facilities are the only answer for IoT security attacks.

2.1.3 SECURITY ISSUES RELATED TO CYBERSECURITY AND IOT

From the earlier discussion, it comes to know that the IoT devices are as on date got no escape from attacks and threats as no devices in the world whether it is of software or hardware in nature is not fully foolproof, as normally said once a password is generated, 50% of security is compromised in that context the IoT devices also prone to various attacks.

As we know that IoT devices are used in real-time applications so associated general problem includes the question of whether IoT systems perform with fast changing real-time data or not.

And also, remote monitoring, machine-to-machine communication areas, and the IoT offer gathering valuable business data. Preventing downtime and offering highly sustained performance are the sought-after requirements, here also the able performance of IoT devices to be verified fully.

It is well known that IoT without computers and networks functionally is not useful in today's world, and at the same time, the problems associated with the computer networks and security issues will automatically be embedded with IoT systems. Also, the various security issues, including attacks and threats, have to be addressed seriously because IoT devices are used in industrial, defense, aerospace, agriculture, pharmaceutical as well as home security.

Another interesting fact is single software platform by the vendors cannot be useful for IoT systems as the customers belong to various unique business patterns, so different software platforms for different customer applications cause tedious system issues, including nonavailability of universal security systems for IoT. Similarly, to reduce the operating and installation cost and interoperability conditions, shared network systems can be used for IoT but it again causes more issues related to mismatching of systems outputs and control issues.

In general, cybercrime causes not only financial losses but also loss to human life, loss of personal information, etc. but can also be possible in IoT system environment, as the number of IoT devices and systems are growing rapidly, as on date, even around 90% of the companies cannot identify that their IoT devices were hacked. The IoT devices, including IP cameras, routers, smart locks, and doors, are susceptible to hacking and attacks.

The IoT attack may be local or global, but till date, nobody estimated how much loss happened to the industry or individual because as on date, the IoT industry is still in its beginning stage—nobody knows its vulnerabilities and strength. Various risks in IoT include authentication problems, authorization problems, device updating disruptions, DDoS attacks, IoT botnet problems, password secrecy, encryption problems and limitations, and security aspects and its limitations.

2.2   FUTURE TRENDS IN CYBERSECURITY RELATED TO IOT

Protecting, managing, and defending the sensitive data in IoT environment are a challenging task as software and hardware of IoT devices are susceptible to severe attacks from outside communication channels or through Internet.

As we know that IoT communication is also done with mobiles and, in most instances, IoT devices are handled, monitored, and controlled by mobile devices, mobiles are easily hacked and compromised, which clearly shows that IoT devices are definitely vulnerable. In a few instances, the selection of IoT devices and gadgets is purely based on economy factor that means cheap cost. Many times in small companies and home automation and controlling situations, people stress more on cheap devices especially IP cameras, which can easily be compromised, and the damage and loss caused by such vulnerable and cheap devices is a perennial problem in IoT security.

It is estimated that the main vulnerable component is IP camera, and next is smart hubs and related storage devices, and still, the research is going on about finding vulnerability parameters of IoT devices. Another drawback of IoT security issues is cloud-based system environment, as we are aware that once the system becomes multidisciplinary in nature, one vulnerability leads to multiple vulnerable weak points for the other stages or systems, so the security issues coupled many fold in various aspects like sensor security, cloud security, network security computer security, botnet problems, etc.

The main problem with IoT devices is password and authentication, as these are used by general public as well. In near future, the password mechanism is to be made as much as simple, and contradictorily, it leads to breaking of passwords easily by hackers. Another serious problem with these devices is easy downloading of malicious programs and software by the users who are not able to identify between good software and malicious software. This leads to direct malfunctioning of devices enabled by IoT, and effect and damages are enormous if these malicious software were planted by hackers or criminals to remotely control the devices, and at the end, it became Internet of cybercrimes than IoT.

The research and development is also on anvil, wherein artificial intelligence, robotics, fuzzy logic, blockchain technology, DevOps, cloud computing, cyber-physical systems, data mining systems, big data analytics, drone technologies, nanotechnology, wireless sensor networks, biosensors, agile, business analytics, sensor technologies, etc. are all getting integrated in one way or another way with IoT, which is broadening the application areas of IoT devices as we have seen at the beginning, IoT devices in general were seen as switch on–switch off systems or opening or closing the door or turning on/off the fan or cooler etc., but, the time has seriously changed in such a way that IoT are now not only used in home automation but also entered in office automation, industrial automation, vehicles, processes, financial platforms, etc. We cannot imagine where there is no IoT. It is well-known fact that an ordinary mobile now contains at least four-to-five sensor-based features that indirectly associated with IoT concept.

At present, we can find four types of IoT platforms, connectivity platform, end-to-end platform, data type platform, and cloud platform.

The general architecture of connectivity IoT platform includes intelligent devices with internal LAN connected to cloud through WAN and multiple users are connected to cloud using WAN. Here intelligent devices from mobile, ad hoc components, etc. help a number of users to access the intelligent devices through cloud. Similarly, in end-to-end platform systems, it connects, manages, and provides facilities for billions of devices and gateways, and with all the possible security features. In the IoT cloud architecture, the connectivity between all user's cloud computing and related data processing can be achieved.

The future of IoT technology is very bright, as the world is changing so fast and people want to handle various data systems and gadgets from distance, and the demand related to IoT product manufacturing, marketing, supply, service, research and development, consultancy, etc. will be drastically increasing 2020 onwards—it is the trend of IoT.

2.3   CONCLUSION

In conclusion, IoT is the new mantra in present world, all big companies are spending billions of dollars into research, development, manufacturing, and marketing of IoT product and solutions, At the same time, the cautious steps are also to be taken in solving potential security threats, attacks and compromising the IoT devices by unsecured hands. Protecting the devices from hackers and various known and unknown attacks is the point of the day. Developing robust IoT system that can work in various platforms simultaneously in real system environment is a challenge.

Protecting against cybercriminals is a herculean task as the technology change is so rapid that every day new features are added, new devices are developed, so another challenge of IoT devices is sustainability and long-run usage. Nowadays, electronic products come with a tagline of "use and throw," and many times whole circuitry for simplicity, saving space and more economical, fabricated on board and offers no serviceable parts in it; all these look like the facility comes cheaply, but in the long run maintenance and other costs will become more. Frequent change in technology offers regular changing of devices and systems that will become more expenditure.

In order to use IoT technology, a practical approach and real-time analysis of the environment where IoT systems are installed is to be done meticulously, expecting sabotage and hacking suitable latest software and hardware security systems to be incorporated at all the levels of IoT environment. The users and people who are using the IoT system must be sanitized so that the attacks should not happen by the insider.

Considering all abovementioned measures, IoT systems can be successfully installed and operated without glitch in all related environments.

KEYWORDS

- **IoT**
- **analysis**
- **network security**
- **cryptography**

REFERENCES

1. Beach, P. M.; Logan, O.; et al. Analysis of Systems Security Engineering Design Principles for the Development of Secure and Resilient Systems. *IEEE Access* 2019.
2. Aldaej, A. Enhancing Cyber Security in Modern Internet of Things Using Intrusion Prevention Algorithm for IoT. *Digital Object Identifier*; 10.1109/ACCESS.2017
3. Lai, R.; Qiu, X.; et al. Robustness of Asymmetric Cyber-Physical Power Systems against Cyber Attacks. *Digital Object Identifier*; 10.1109/ACCESS.2019.2915927; May 22, 2019.
4. Abomhara, M.; Køien, G. M. Cyber Security and the Internet of Things: Vulnerabilities, Threats, Intruders and Attacks. 2015; RP_Journal_2245-1439_414.pdf
5. Siboni, S.; Sachidananda, V.; et al. Security Testbed for Internet-of-Things Devices. *IEEE Trans. Reliab.* **2019**, *68* (1).
6. Musaddiq, A.; Zikria, Y. B.; et al. A Survey on Resource Management in IoT Operating Systems AR. *Digital Object Identifier*; 10.1109/ACCESS.2018.2808324; February 21, 2018.
7. Hassan, A. M.; Awad, A. I. Urban Transition in the Era of the Internet of Things: Social Implications and Privacy Challenges. *Digital Object Identifier*; 10.1109/ACCESS.2018.2838339; July 19, 2018.

CHAPTER 3

Applications of IoT in Medical Technology and Healthcare

PARSHANT KUMAR SHARMA[1,2*], SHRADDHA KAUSHIK[3*],
SAURABH PANDEY[4], MEGHA GUPTA[3], NISHANT VATS[5],
MANU GAUTAM[6], and MADHUSUDAN SHARMA[7,8]

[1]*Department of Electrical Engineering, Kwangwoon University, Seoul, South Korea*

[2]*VBRI Innovation Pvt. Ltd., New Delhi, India*

[3]*Department of Biotechnology, Institute of Engineering and Technology (IET), Lucknow, Uttar Pradesh, India*

[4]*Department of Biotechnology, S. D. College of Engineering & Technology, Muzaffarnagar, Uttar Pradesh, India*

[5]*Department Production Planning and Control; Varroc Polymers India Pvt. Ltd., Greater Noida, Uttar Pradesh, India*

[6]*Department of Biosciences, Shri Ram College, Muzaffarnagar, Uttar Pradesh, India*

[7]*Bayer Crop Science Limited, Uttar Pradesh, India*

[8]*Bayer Crop Science, Germany*

Corresponding author. E-mail: parshantvats111@gmail.com; shraddhakaushik97@gmail.com

ABSTRACT

We will be the witness for the future applications of healthcare that would take place through Hi-tech technologies, such as AI, VR/AR, 3D printing, robotics, or nanotechnology. We have to familiarize ourselves with the latest developments in order to control technology, rather not the other way around. Now healthcare has come across to prominent changes because of its dramatic technology developments, from antibiotics, anesthetics to magnetic MRI scanners, and radiotherapy. Innovation in future technology is continued to keep metamorphoses in the health-care sector, yet while technologies (new drugs and treatments, new devices, new social media support for healthcare, etc.) will drive innovation, but the human factors will remain one of the stable limitations of breakthroughs. This chapter highlights the fragments for the future to get the information more clearly about how to get, where we want to go, and we will look at the pros and cons of technology in medical and their relationship to both patients and professionals alike. The Internet of things seems to be the prominent solution to attenuate the pressures on health-care systems because of its eye-catcher of much recent research.

3.1   INTRODUCTION

Internet of things (IoT) is a new emerging technology of the Internet. It has played a major role in environmental effects and concerns with a variety of nonwired and wired connections that are combinedly working to develop an application for a new service and achieve a similar goal.

For the last few decades, the Internet evolution showed that new approaches toward technologies can affect all aspects of businesses. Worldwide communication is always possible with the help of new innovations such as network connections, wireless communication, and sensors. IoT provided a new, positive path for the business that has been accepted by the business owners and introduced it as new solutions in information and communication technology (ICT) that, they believe, has the capacity to earn a great and valuable income.

The aim of IoT is to permit the objects for connection at anytime, anywhere with anything, and any person who gets the quintessential use of any route, service, or network. Various countries such as the United States, China, European, and India have many simulations to support IoT. IoT European Research Cluster reported three stimulations, for the enhancement of IoT in countries is economic success, quality of life, and environmental protection.

A considerable amount of this research looks at monitoring patients with specific conditions, such as diabetes.[1] Further research looks to serve specific purposes, such as aiding rehabilitation through constant monitoring of a patient's progress.[2] Emergency healthcare has also been recognized as a possibility by related works[3,4] but has not yet been widely researched. Several connected works have been examined in the last specific areas and automation related to IoT healthcare.

An extensive survey is presented with focus placed on commercially available solutions, possible applications, and remaining problems.[5] Each topic is contemplated separately, in lieu of part of an overarching system.[6] Sensor types are compared by Xu et al.[7] with some focus placed on communications.

Medical technologies are products, services, or solutions used to save and improve people's lives. When you are unwell, diagnostics and medical devices help health-care professionals restore you to good health as quickly as possible.[8] I honestly believe that this is the only way forward. Technology can only help to improve our lives, if we use it properly, then we are always (at least) two steps ahead it. But if we restrict to this rule, then the amazing results will be achieved by the cooperation between people and technology. These results will be in medicine and healthcare, and advanced technology could help alchemize unsustainable health-care systems into sustainable ones, by equating the relationship between medical professionals and patients Results are cheaper, faster, and more effective solutions for diseases—automation could lead to better path to cure cancer, AIDS, or Ebola and could simply lead to healthier individuals living in healthier communities.[9] But as the saying goes, one has to be a master of his own house, so it is worth starting "the future" with the betterment of our own health through digital technologies and changing our own attitude toward the concept of health as such and toward medicine and healthcare.[10] The medical culture is similar—there have been prominent technological changes, and actually these changes would be tough to understand and explain.

Does anybody even know how an infusion pump works? They were designed to be clockwork (and before that, gravity fed) and now almost everything contains a digital and colorful screen with lots of keywords to use. Implanted defibrillators are the instruments with an updated automation that use telephone networks and websites to keep cardiologists up-to-date with their patients and this technique is just an amaze; new pharmaceuticals change moods, change blood pressure, or kill bacteria: All are modern mesmerizing magic.

On mirroring, given the centuries of stability, it is wonderful to see how much healthcare has changed in the last 150 years—and one amazing is that how this era with acceleration will proceed in the future.[11]

Author C. Clarke, the prolific futurist and science fiction writer, famously said that any sufficiently advanced technology is indistinguishable from magic. Perhaps the main difference for the pair lifted out of the 19th century is they are suit's magic, whereas we have stopped thinking about it, and just take it for granted.[11] Some of today's advancement such as science fiction is going to be regime in the future, perhaps even in our lifetimes. Yet story about relationships, hopes, error, grief, and denial is going to remain entirely recognizable in the future.

IoT will help in overcoming various controversies such as authority gradient, human error, and patients, who are still helpless, to be treated easily. The reason is that market controls the automation: If anyone has design to that they can into a physical realization that they can sell, they can also file patent for it or license it thereby making a revenue on their stake.

To improve the culture, this will encourage them to find ways of making it cheaper and smaller and to market it on a very large scale. Unlikely, the human culture does not make the profit for anybody. To improve the culture, admitting some processes which are not good enough to start with and for those who want to follow it, especially the lawyers, re-watching the processes can act as a little incentive.[6] There are more than 500,000 medical technologies available in hospitals, community-care settings, and at home (https://www.medtecheurope.org/about-the-industry/what-is-medical-technology). Medical technology can be an everyday object such as latex gloves, sticking plasters, cancer screening tests, or syringes.

It could also be the hearing aids, spectacles, pregnancy tests, or wheelchairs. Medical technologies allow individuals to live longer and better lives. Medical technologies also empower people to contribute the society for longer. In doing so, they improve the sustainability of health-care systems and the quality of care.

In its many forms, medical technology is beneficial to the health and quality of life.

Medical technology offers (https://www.medtecheurope.org/about-the-industry/what-is-medical-technology) the following.

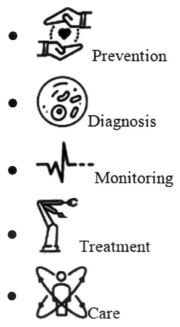

- Prevention

- Diagnosis

- Monitoring

- Treatment

- Care

There are three main categories of medical technologies:

✓ Medical devices
✓ In vitro diagnostics
✓ Digital health solutions

3.2 INTERNET OF THINGS (IOT) IN HEALTHCARE

IoT helps in monitoring the patient in nonclinical environments such as at home with the help of the technology. Moreover, it will help in reducing strain on hospital resources such as doctors and beds. It is an emerging scope to provide better access to healthcare for those living in the rural areas and can give people better control over their own health.

IoT has some cons as well and the most notable disadvantage is security risk as IoT provides big data collection that contains large amount of sensitive data stored in a single database. The development of IoT healthcare systems is for specific purposes, including assisted ambient living, rehabilitation, and diabetes management for elder patients, and more.

3.2.1   IMPACT OF TECHNOLOGY IN HEALTHCARE

There are no other ways about it: Technological developments in health-care have saved innumerous patients and are continuously improving our quality of life. Not only that, but also technology in the medical field had a massive impact on nearly all processes and practices of health-care professionals.[12]

3.2.2   DIGITALIZATION OF HEALTH RECORDS

Electronic health records (EHRs) replaced the outdated paper records that have been a massive game changer for everybody in this medical world. In industry-wide implementation, the medical assistant to professionals of medical coding to registered nurses is just a helpful role that has been impacted by this.

Not only can patients access their records at the click of a button, but it also ensured that mistakes are caught more quickly (without needing to pore over unreadable physicians' handwriting). Nurses and technicians are responsible for inputting patient data into a central, digitized system. Medical billers and coders update patient records with diagnostic codes (such as test results) and submit medical claims to insurance companies.[12]

There are many benefits that EHR has brought to healthcare, which are described in the following sections.

3.2.3   GREATER PATIENT CARE

EHR can automatically alert the treating physician to potential issues (such as intolerances to certain medicines or allergies). EHRs can be accessed by any medical facility, which is extremely useful for doctors to assess nonlocal patients (and it very crucial if the patient is unresponsive).[12]

3.2.4   IMPROVED PUBLIC HEALTH

EHRs provide invaluable data to the clinical researchers, helping them to advance the medical knowledge and the development of treatments for the common health problems (like viral outbreaks).

A standardized health IT system can provide the insights into how the widespread and outbreaks are enabling preventative measures (such as increased flu shot production) to be put in place much more quickly.

3.2.5   EASE OF WORKFLOW

The introduction of EHRs has only made the life easier for medical billers and coders. Entering data into a computerized system is much a less time-consuming than paper-based methods, and it reduces the risk of errors in patient data and financial details. Digitally accessing patient records also allows medical coding experts to work from home, increasing its efficiency and the productivity.[12]

3.2.6   LOWER HEALTH-CARE COSTS

According to a study from the University of Michigan, shifting from paper to EHRs reduced the cost of the outpatient care by 3%. These researchers estimated that $5.14 are being saved by each patient in each month. In a large city hospital network, that amount is incalculable.[12]

3.2.7   REHABILITATION

The quite interesting topic of researchers in this field is rehabilitation after physical injury. On the basis of the individual's symptoms, a system has been developed that generates a rehabilitation plan tailored to an individual based on their symptoms. This system compares the patient's condition with a database of patients' previous symptoms, ailments, and treatments to achieve this. Approval of the recommended treatment has to fill manually by the doctors; 87.9% of cases have been approved by the doctor and agreed completely with the system, and no modifications were made to the treatment plan it proposed. A mathematical model for the measurement of joint angles in physical hydrotherapy systems is proposed, which permits the improvement of joint movement to be tracked through therapy.

3.2.8   IOT IN PARKINSON'S MONITORING

IoT technologies played an important role in the evaluation for their usefulness in a system for monitoring patients suffering from Parkinson's disease. They made a conclude disease; wearable sensors for observing the tremors, gait patterns, and general activity levels which could be used in combination with the vision-based technologies (i.e., cameras) around the home. Furthermore, the authors suggest the machine learning could help in future in the advancement in the treatment plans.

3.2.9   DETECTING BLOOD-GLUCOSE LEVEL

A laboratory protocol for the monitoring of blood-glucose levels in diabetic patients was proposed in a study. System works in three following steps:

I.   First patients have to manually take blood-glucose level at defined intervals.
II. Then two types of blood-glucose abnormality will be considered. The first is abnormal blood-glucose levels and the second is a missed blood-glucose reading.
III. Then the system itself analyzes the severity of abnormality and will decide how to notify the patient themselves, family members and caregivers, or emergency health-care providers such as doctors.

This system has practical approach and has been proven realizable, though further improvements could be made by the automating blood-glucose measurements.

3.2.10   DETECTING CARDIAC ARREST

A system used in detecting heart attacks with the help of ready-made components and a custom antenna. To measure the heart activity, an electrocardiogram (ECG) sensor is used, which is processed by a micro-controller. User gets this information on his smartphone by the help of Bluetooth, and after that, ECG data is further processed and is submitted in a user application. The authors spotted that prediction of developing heart attack would improve by the system software. By measuring the respiratory rate, further modifications could be made, which is known a prior symptom in the prediction of heart attack. SPHERE is a system that utilizes vision-based (i.e., camera) wearable and environmental sensors for general the activity and for maintaining health monitoring purposes. To allow older and chronically ill patients to live in the comfort of their own homes, and their monitoring will be under remote healthcare is the main aim of this project. This allows the involvement of caretakers and doctors if any issues arise. Recent studies have shown that machine learning would be beneficial for learning about conditions and for making decisions about the patient's healthcare (Fig. 3.1).[13]

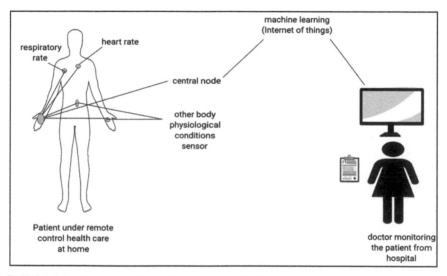

FIGURE 3.1   Schematic illustration of IoT application in medical healthcare.

3.3   COMPONENTS OF IOT MODEL

3.3.1   WEARABLE SENSORS AND CENTRAL NODES

Physiological conditions of the body such as temperature pressure are measured by the wearable sensors and central nodes. The most utilizable sensors are those which measure pulse, respiratory rate, and body temperature as these show the important changes in determination of the health conditions. Nowadays, to monitor or to check blood pressure and blood oxygen, sensors are used. Joint angle sensors, blood-glucose, and fall detection have been instrumented for the specific conditions. Sensor nodes give the signal to the central node.

3.3.2   SHORT-RANGE COMMUNICATION

To send the signal to the central node, a communication method is required, that is, short-range communication method. Several things have to be kept in mind while choosing the short-range communication method: Effect on human body; there should be no harmful effect on the human body. Risk security must be concern to ensure the data is safe. Computing is essential to overcome the delay for time-critical system.[1]

3.3.3   LONG-TERM COMMUNICATION

As sensor is received by the central node, the data would not be worth unless it will not reach the doctors or caretakers safely. In long-term communication, several things have to keep in mind such as security, error correction, robustness against interference, low latency, and high availability. High-quality error correction, robustness against interference, and low latency are crucial as to provide ease in message sending and receiving. High availability is essential as no matter where the patient is located, message should be delivered all the time.[1]

3.3.4   SECURE CLOUD STORAGE ARCHITECTURE AND MACHINE LEARNING

It is beneficial for the doctors to know the patient's medical history.[14] Based on literature, cloud storage is most effective for storage purposes.[14] As machine learning is not effective unless large databases of information are available.[15] To improve health-care system, machine learning is a boon. Machine learning provides effective method to identify previously unknown data, give treatment and diagnostic plans, and recommend to the doctors which is individual patient specific. To implement machine learning, cloud storage architecture should be designed (Fig. 3.2).[2,16]

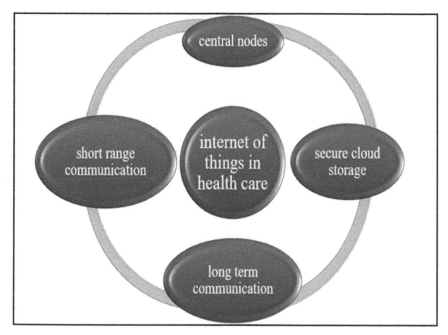

FIGURE 3.2   Pictorial representation for components of IoT model.

3.4   IOT IN CLOUD COMPUTING

3.4.1   *BIG DATA AND THE CLOUD*

The term "big data" refers to enormous amounts of data, which are collected, processed, and used for analytics. When the data is analyzed by the experts, the information of it has their multiple benefits, such as reducing health-care costs, predicting epidemics, avoiding preventable deaths, improving quality of life, reducing health-care waste, developing new drugs and treatments, and improving the efficiency and quality of care.[12] Healthcare stores huge amounts of data of every single second (one research study can amount to 100 TB of data), so these facilities will require safe storage solutions, expandable, and cost-effective. To deliver services across the Internet, cloud then uses hardware and software.[12]

3.4.2 BETTER AND SAFER DATA STORAGE

For the data storage as safer and better, cloud computer technology allows the masses of information to be stored in a very low cost, all without any additional hardware or server or any limitations (and expenses). Cloud storage will protect against all the loss sensitive data with their strong backups and their recovery services with an increased reliance or HR systems.[12]

3.4.3 IMPROVED ACCESS TO BIG DATA

The cloud is an invaluable tool for medical research and sharing medical information. From mobilizing workforces to sharing big data to improve the accuracy of research studies, this full range of functions is changing the medical landscape.[12]

3.4.4 DANGERS ASSOCIATED WITH ARTIFICIAL INTELLIGENCE IN MEDICINE

We cannot deny that there are many advantages of technologies in healthcare, but there are a handful of issues that require attention.[12]

3.4.5 CENTRALIZED DATA POINT

Centralized data point is a central point of all the data information that is extremely useful, but if there is any connectivity or band with problems or overdependence that may result in serious repercussions.[12] However, the main concern rising from increased mobile use and cloud computing technology is data protection and security.[12]

3.4.6 THE RISK OF MEDICAL RECORDS HACKING

In 2015, in Anthem, which is the second-largest health insurance company in the United States, almost 80 million records were stolen by the hackers. In this, the names and addresses were stolen (no details regarding the illness or treatments of patients were exposed), but then the question rises if this can occur to an insurance giant such as Anthem, how safe the patient's records were in local clinics? Patient records apparently being a big business, about 10 or 20 times the value of a credit card number with stolen health credentials fetch more than $10 each. This information of the stolen records can be used for making the fake ID's (to purchase the drugs/medical equipment's or for to submit the false insurance claims).[13]

3.4.7   INFORMATION AND COMMUNICATION TECHNOLOGY

ICT linked health-care professionals and professional with the patients. Telemonitoring systems, smartphones, and e-mails are all useful for more rural areas and locations with a lack of facilities and/or specialists and are also used to share information.[13]

3.4.8   TELEMEDICINE

The terms "telemedicine" and "telehealth" can be used to refer to two-way video consultations (or the transmission of health-care data like ECGs). Telemedicine can be used in many fields, especially in a sector like cardio-vascular healthcare.[12]

Telemonitoring technology can monitor blood levels, symptoms, and vital signs of blood levels from a remote location. Future cardiac monitor technicians will be happy to learn that AliveCor is developing a device to detect potassium blood levels to prevent hyperkalemia. Till now not been approved by the FDA, but this is a suitable example to show how technology is helping in the needs of at-risk patients.[12] Telehealth has improvised a lot and continue to improve in allied health-care jobs, including some of the high-salary roles in the area. The implementation of these telemedicine options means less crowded of patients in waiting rooms and less pressure on front desk teams.[12]

3.5   MOBILE APP TECHNOLOGY IN THE MEDICAL FIELD

Mobile health apps offer greater flexibility to all parties. They are one of the most inexpensive ways for facilities to provide stronger services to their patients.[12]

Some work to create better health awareness while others facilitate communication between patient and care providers. Some of the areas that "m-health" apps assist include as follows:

- Chronic care management
- Medication management
- Medical reference
- Diagnostics
- Personal health records
- Women's health
- Fitness and weight-loss
- Mental health

Other benefits include as follows:

- Shorter patient waiting times
- Improved access in rural areas
- Improved efficiency, leading to savings

3.6   CRYPTOGRAPHY IN HEALTHCARE

Cryptography in health-care system Internet has been made an ease for the faster transmission of image, videos, text, and any valuable information. But in the era of digitalization, cybercrime has been increased. So, these valuable information needs throughout encryption that cannot be decoded by any third party rather than receiver and sender.

Medical images are highly usable in various fields such as medical science, military communication, biometric field, medical imaging, telemedicine, and online photo albums. Three-step security is required to secure medical images

   a. Confidentiality: To maintain the security of information between a sender and receiver. No third person could access that information.
   b. Integrity: The data should be same during and after transmission.
   c. Availability: Data should be easily accessible to the authorized person.

Encryption is needed for the safely transmission of the images and text. Statistics are required to be encrypted so that no unauthorized person could gain access. Ways of encryption of images and text both are different. The encryption for image is quite different because an image has big functionality, high redundancy, and correlation between the pixels. For the encryption of data, various mathematical algorithms and keys are used. And then for the decryption of the coded data to recover the original facts, various mathematical algorithms and keys are used. To encrypt the text, data block or stream ciphers are directly used because text is a sequence of words, while to encrypt the image, 2D array must be converted into 1D array. To represent the digital image, 2D arrays are used. Image compression is required during encryption and decryption to reduce the storage space and transmission time.

3.6.1 CRYPTOGRAPHIC TERMINOLOGY

Plaintext: The source message. Ciphertext: The distorted message.

Key: Critical statistics utilized by the cipher, only the exporter and importer recognize the key. Cipher: a bonanza rule for remodeling decoded to coded text. Code: the method of converting plaintext into ciphertext using algorithms. Encipher: (encrypt) converting unencrypted text to encrypted text by the usage of a cipher and a key.

Decipher: (decrypt) converting ciphertext into plaintext the usage of a cipher and a key. Cryptology: the combination of cryptography and cryptanalysis. Cryptography: study of encryption principles and strategies. Cryptanalysis: (code breaking) the look at of standards and techniques of decoding codes without knowing a key.

Hash algorithm: An algorithmic rule that converts textual content into a string of fixed length. Secret key cryptography: Single key is used for both enciphering and deciphering. Public key cryptography: Two keys are used—one key for encryption and some other for decode. Public key infrastructure (PKI): PKI is a certification authority.

3.6.2 CRYPTOGRAPHIC ALGORITHMS

This type of algorithm depends upon the number of keys used. Cryptographic algorithms can be categorized into two types:

1. Symmetric algorithms (secret key)
2. Asymmetric algorithms (public key)

Symmetric: It is also known as secret key or private key. Sender and receiver used a single key for decode and encode. Examples: data encryption standard (DES), triple DES, and advanced encryption standard (AES). Asymmetric: Two different keys (public and private keys) are used for enciphering and deciphering. For encipher, public key is used. For decipher, private key is used. Examples: Rivest–Shamir–Adleman and Elliptic curve cryptosystem (ECC). Encryption algorithm: encipher message created as output. Enciphered data depends on the plaintext and the secret key. It performs various addition and deletion on the ASCII. Decryption algorithm: opposite of encoding.

To get plaintext as an output requires codes and secret keys as an input. An encipher algorithm for interactive media data based on arithmetic modulo. Both coded text and clear text are of block size 64. 64-bit length is for secret key. The structure of this block cipher provides confusion and diffusion.[17]

3.7   LITERATURE SURVEY

Natsheh et al.[18] have presented an algorithm using XOR cipher with AES.

DICOM stands for Digital Images and Communication in Medicine. This file contains two parts: header data and client data. Header data (textual data) stores the patient's information. Name, scan image type, and pixel array attributes such as pixel depth are required for clinical data. Pixel data contains an image, short video or audio. DICOM gives confidentiality for header records.

DICOM supports the huge kind of digital medical images consisting of computed tomography (CT), and MRI. Medical images are required greater computational time to encode and decode. In this chapter, AES used for only one image is an encoded and XOR codes for encrypting the remaining multiframe DICOM images.

XOR cipher: A symmetric algorithm for encoding. Boolean algebra is used for the development of XOR codes. XOR function is to give "true," while two arguments have different values. XOR function can be applied to binary bits. In enciphering, the strength of the XOR codes depends on the length and the nature of the key. Lengthy key achieves higher overall performance.

XOR-AES–based encryption: First approach: First image should be in the multiframe DICOM images because XOR codes are required to encode the rest of the images in the multiframes. Second approach: Use AES with Counter (CTR) mode of operation to encode the keys, for the evaluation of this algorithm entropy, computational time, normalized correlation, PSNR (peak signal to noise ratio), and histogram analysis.

Medical image confidentiality was achieved by using the XOR cipher. The XOR keys were generated randomly. The approach of encryption is based on a random key that shows shorter encryption and better performance, new approach than decode timing.

Kushwaha et al.[19] have proposed a new automation that shows both encryption and watermarking for the safe transaction of medical image.

In this scheme, for watermark, region of interest (ROI) image is used. Linear-feedback shift registers totally and stream ciphering is used to encode selected ROI portion. Again, to encode this portion, public keys are used. That key is derived from a Diffie–Hellman algorithm. ROI is embedded into the medical image by spread spectrum scheme.

Bit plane slicing: To analyze the image, keeping apart a digital image into bit planes, every pixel is of 8 bits. Suppose, the image has eight 1-bit planes. It has the ranges from bit plane 1–0 (LSB) to bit plane 7 (MSB). Bit plane 0 includes all decreasing order bits and bit plane 7 includes all increasing order bits.

Bit plane extraction for an image of 8-bit value lies 0 and 127 for gray-level transformation maps to one level and from 129 to 253 to another for maps all level.

Diffie–Hellman: It is the path of exchanging cryptographic keys. It allows two persons who do not have any kind of information about each other. They shared their confidential key through the information super-highway. That clue is used to encode the medical image.

For example, S and R are sender and receiver, then S and R agree a secret key. m and n are two large numbers m and n such that $1 < n < m$. S chooses random A and then computes $A = $ na mod m. R chooses random B and then computes $B = $ nb mod m. S computes Key1 $= $ na mod m. R computes Key2 $= $ nb mod m. Key1 $= $ Key2 $= $ nab mod m.

Watermarking: It is the process of planting digital statistics into another for copyright protection, authentication, and authorized verification. For encipher, use the equation $E = S(h, m, k)$, where E is the Stego image, h

is the host image, m is the watermark image, and k are a secret key. For deciphering, use the equation $D (E, k)$.

Encryption: Using bit plane slicing, MSB plane will be chosen from the medical image, and then select the ROI from the plane MSB. Generate a 64-bit secret key the use of LFSR and added to each pixel of the image. Using Diffie–Hellman algorithm, the public key is generated.

Decryption: Choose encoded watermark image for extraction. Stream cipher will be used for the decoding of the watermarked image. Public key will be generated by using Diffie–Hellman algorithm. Add it to extract pixel of the encoded image. Finally, the ROI image is obtained. The different medical images are tested by using this scheme. It may be MRI, CT scan, and X-ray images.

In this chapter, MRI of size 256 × 256 was taken as cover image and ROI of the image is taken as watermark. The public key is generated via using a D–H algorithm by growing the level of security.

C. Simranjeet Kaur et al. introduced a new reversible data hiding technique for authentication and data hiding.

In this chapter, ROI and non-ROI (NROI) is defined. ROI is protected and efforts embed data in NROI. Here, semireversible scheme is capable of hiding patient's data. The fragile watermarking technique is used to verify authenticity of the image, to achieve image authentication.

Watermark: Using hash function, generate a fixed hexadecimal number message to a particular message defined by the sender. Read the text file. It contains patient's information and converted character into integer values. Embedding the watermark in:

NROI steps: (1) MATLAB environment is required to READ the image. (2) Then image will be converted into gray scale. (3) Separate of ROI and NROI will be performed using the cropping tool. (4) Examine diagnosis report. (5) Generation of watermark by combining steps (3) and (4). (6) Put the integer form of concatenated character string data into an array called TABLE . (7) Cross-check the host image from the table and match for minimum difference match in NROI. (8) Confirm its location in a secret key array. (9) Update the encrypted image array according to this newly found pixel and update the secret key. (10) The watermarked signal image will be produced.

Extraction process: (1) Load the watermarked image. (2) Extract the pixels by using the secret key in the sequence provided by secret key and put it in an array. (3) Decrypt the extracted watermark. (4) Compute the

MAC code. (5) Compare the extracted hashes to the computed hash. (6) If both are same, then received image is authentic. (7) If both are not the same, then received image is unauthentic. To evaluate the performance, DICOM image of brain of patient was used.

Fragile data hiding technique preserves the record of medical image through embedding the medical diagnosis report and other records. This approach lets in the storing and transmission of electronic patient record besides image authentication codes. The original image can be recovered perfectly. The scheme is good at authentication. (8) Disadvantages of EHRs—theoretically, shifting to EHRs should change everything for the better.

Unfortunately, there are some disadvantages that still need to be work out on that. Rather than a records system that works fluidly, many miscommunications between one another.

Sometimes, this lack of these machinery developments provides countless benefits, and the primary concern is providing better communication and interaction between doctor and patient.

Studies, however, state that artificial intelligence would be able to overcome this communication gap between doctor and patient.

Open hidden challenges, but the data is promising.[12]

KEYWORDS

- **3D printing**
- **future technology**
- **healthcare**
- **innovation**
- **human factors**
- **Internet of things**

REFERENCES

1. Baker, S. B.; Xiang, W.; Atkinson, I. M. Internet of Things for Smart Healthcare: Technologies, Challenges, and Opportunities. *IEEE Access* **2017,** *5,* 26521–26544.
2. Chang, S. H.; Chiang, R. D.; Wu, S. J.; Chang, W. T. A Context-Aware, Interactive M-Health System for Diabetics. *IT Prof.* **2016,** *18,* 14–22.

3. Pasluosta, C. F.; Gassner, H.; Winkler, J.; Klucken, J.; Eskoer, B. M. An Emerging Era in the Management of Parkinson's Disease: Wearable Technologies and the Internet of Things. *Biomed. Health Inform.* **2015**, *19*, 1873–1881.
4. Fan, Y. J.; Yin, Y. H.; Xu, L. D.; Zeng, Y.; Wu, F. IoT-Based Smart Rehabilitation System. *IEEE Trans. Ind. Inform.* **2014**, *10*, 1568–1577.
5. Yin, Y.; Zeng, Y.; Chen, X.; Fan, Y. The Internet of Things in Healthcare: An Overview. *J. Ind. Inf. Integr.* **2016**, *1*, 3–13.
6. Dimitrov, D. V. Medical Internet of Things and Big Data in Healthcare. *Healthcare Inform. Res.* **2016**, *22*, 156–163.
7. Xu, B.; Xu, L. D.; Cai, H.; Xie, C.; Hu, J.; Bu, F. Ubiquitous Data Accessing Method in IoT-Based Information System for Emergency Medical Services. *IEEE Trans. Ind. Inform..* **2014**, *10*, 17578–17586.
8. Pasluosta, C. F.; Gassner, H.; Winkler, J.; Klucken, J.; Eskoer, B. M. An Emerging Era in the Management of Parkinson's Disease: Wearable Technologies and the Internet of Things. *Biomed. Health Inform.* **2015**, *19*, 1873–1881.
9. Mesko, B. *The Medical Futurist Institute Block*; 2017.
10. Meskó, B.; Drobni, Z.; Bényei, E.; Gergely, B.; Győrffy, Z. Digital Health is a Cultural Transformation of Traditional Healthcare. *mHealth* **2017**, *3*, 38 (1–8).
11. Thimbleby, H. Technology and the Future of Healthcare. *J. Public Health Res.* **2013**, *2*, e28 (1–11).
12. Banova, B. The Impact of Technology in Healthcare. *Am. Inst. Med. Sci. Educ. (AIMSE)* **2019**.
13. Alansari, Z.; Soomro, S.; Belgaum, M. R. The Rise of Internet of Things (IoT) in Big Healthcare Data: Review and Open Research Issues. *Progr. Adv. Comput. Intell. Eng.* **2016**, *2*.
14. Olaronke, I.; Oluwaseun, O. Big Data in Healthcare: Prospects, Challenges and Resolutions. *Proc. Future Technol. Conf. (FTC)* **2016**, 1152–1157.
15. Zhou, J.; Cao, Z.; Dong, X.; Vasilakos, A. V. Security and Privacy for Cloud-Based IoT: Challenges. *IEEE Commun. Mag.* **2017**, *55*, 26–33.
16. Zhu, N.; Diethe, T.; Camplani, M.; Tao, L.; Burrows, A.; Twomey, N.; Kaleshi, D.; Mirmehdi, M.; Flach, P. A.; Craddock, I. Bridging e-Health and the Internet of Things: The SPHERE Project. *IEEE Intell. Syst.* **2015**, *30*, 39–46.
17. Kavitha1, M.; Prathima1, G. S.; Kayalvizhi1, G.; Sanguida1, A.; Ezhumalai, G.; Ramesh, V. Evaluation of Streptococcus Mutans Serotypes e, f, and k in Saliva Samples of 6–12-Year-Old School Children Before and After a Short-Term Daily Intake of the Probiotic Lozenge. *J. Indian Soc. Pedod. Prev. Dent.* **2019**, *37*, 67–74.
18. Natsheh, Q. N.; Li, B.; Gale, A. G. Security of Multi-Frame DICOM Images Using XOR Encryption Approach. *Procedia Comput. Sci.* **2016**, *90*, 175–181.
19. Kushwaha, V. K.; Anusudha, K. ROI Based Double Encryption Approach for Secure Transaction of Medical Images. *Int. J. Adv. Res. Electr. Electron. Instrum. Eng.* **2013**, *2*, 1418–1423.

CHAPTER 4

Design of an IoT-Based Mobile Healthcare Unit Using a Self-regulated React.js Database and Arduino

PUSHAN KUMAR DUTTA[1,*], RITA KARMAKAR[2], RISHABH PIPALWA[3], AVHISHEK ADHIKARY[3], ARNAB CHAKRABORTY[3], and ABHIPSA PATTNAIK[4]

[1]*Amity School of Engineering and Technology, Amity University Kolkata, Kolkata, India*

[2]*Amity Institute of Psychology and Allied Sciences, Amity University Kolkata, Kolkata, India*

[3]*Amity School of Information Technology, Amity University Kolkata, Kolkata, India*

[4]*Bachelor of Business Administration-Information Technology, Symbiosis Institute of Computer Science and Research, Pune, India*

Corresponding author: E-mail: pkdutta@kol.amity.edu

ABSTRACT

In our everyday lives, there is a necessity to get a health checkup on time. Normally medical tests are performed by doctors, while with the advent of modern technology, different diagnostic tests that can be self-performed have come in the market. In the proposed work, we have designed a hardware module that involves integrating sensors that include a pulse oximeter MAX30102: and heart rate monitor module with Arduino UNO board for tracking a patient's electronic medical record. We intend to build a personal assistant–based ecosystem that will help us in keeping track of health by monitoring body using cryptic push–pull modes that are one-step pulses that are stored in crypto and stores tasks such as booking appointments, viewing or reminding booked appointments, keep track of daily medicine prescriptions in a JSON format in React.js Native. In this manner, we aim to develop a self-regulating intake and inventory management of personal medicine in a more nurturing and enjoyable manner.

4.1   INTRODUCTION

There is a need for open, inexpensive, and reliable electronic instruments in this modern era as there is a need for the introduction of new smartphone apps and sensors for healthcare and biomedical research. While many existing software systems provide useful alternatives for both physicians and patients, few apps continue to serve clinical treatment to promote sustainable health. As technology continues to progress, many actions have become automated. Many of the modern-day diseases are lifestyle phenomena, and they have been observed to create adolescents more inactive, increasing the levels of illness in the community. With the modern-age data science and lifestyle enhancing apps on wellness and lifestyle modifications, many of the I-health apps have come in the market range from system apps packaged with the manufacturer's device Fooducate, My Net Diary Calorie Counter PRO, MySugr, Health2Sync, Diabetes Connect, Diabetes: M, OneTouch Reveal to third-party applications (e.g., Runkeeper). In conjunction with mobile apps, dedicated fitness tools like smart watches and Fitbit are available for health support. Data can be transmitted electronically to the Patient Monitoring System using the proposed system, allowing the patient to be tracked consistently. Although not usually detailed, all of these health-related programs rely on phone or wearable live data, such as accelerometers and gyroscopes, to infer details related to health. Ubiquitous technology is present everywhere, and (Dowker, 2019; Gong et al., 2019) the user should use the service. The purpose of this current scheme is to track the patient's body's temperature and heartbeat that should be reflected to the individual being handled using NRF infrastructure. This pervasive technology and well-being interests lead to better life assessment and make a person understand the clinical disorders which are both lifestyle-based and physiological called *U-Health*.

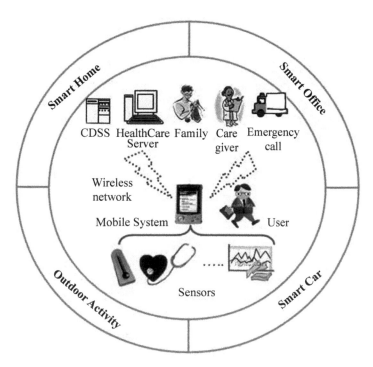

FIGURE 4.1   Applicable U-healthcare.

U-healthcare is shown as a schematic diagram in Figure 4.1. U-Healthcare means that physicians or users can use health services such as diagnostic services, emergency management services, monitoring anywhere (Di Matteo et al., 2018; Wang et al., 2018) at any time. Healthcare registry receives a series of users' health records and saves the data to the database. The database of healthcare also examines the patient's raw data. CDSS (Clinical Decision Support System) is also an appropriate knowledge system that provides case-specific tips incorporating two or even more confidential information items (Love-Koh et al., 2018). CDSS is very useful for bringing on medical experience with patient data and to recommend using the correct inference engine (Türk et al., 2019). Because of the healthcare system, we use the monitoring system to analyze medical information for participants and get guidance from either client on the healthcare database (Gulliver et al., 2019). This kind of lifestyle diseases need a very basic understanding of medical terms and allow reuse of domain knowledge (Gagnon et al., 2015). In the modern era, since there is uncontrolled sugar intake, it can often lead to diabetes and other disorders that can result in uncontrolled blood pressure. With the use of U-Health, the role of diabetes resources in improving self-care habits such as controlling glucose, diet, foot care, and medical behavior can be explored in multiple intervention studies (Kirwan et al., 2013; Nundy et al., 2014; Ruggiero et al., 2014; Sarkar et al., 2016). While many are capable of collecting active (survey) and passive (sensor) information, fewer metadata are available. Metadata can always be categorized as material about an applicant completing a questionnaire or physiological test (e.g., time from each discussion or aim). Our aim is to determine how to send alert warnings to physicians and appropriate connections on certain threshold deviations or taking medication or consuming too much sugar and so on advice, tips, and tricks from online resources to live a healthy life. Enabling people to perform physical activities to keep them away from the major diabetes signs, obesity, and manage premiums to health insurance, renewals, and make medical requests. Socializing with fellow users is based on user patterns/behaviors in general and from those who follow similar habits. Most of these features are data-driven and can be made to evolve with major machine learning and data analysis techniques.

4.1.1   U-HEALTH CARE SYSTEM

Systems design is the process of defining a system's architecture, components, modules, interfaces, and data to meet specific requirements. Using the system design, the overall product architecture, the subsystems that make up the product, and how subsystems are allocated to processors are shown. UML is used for system design modeling. In place of UML logic, we implement a JSON-based cryptic framework of modeling. U-healthcare allows customers and carriers to access medical information about consumers anytime and anywhere. Use of the example of U-healthcare is shown in Figure 4.1. Our key goal is to create an environment that will allow us to be safe and autonomous. When it comes to health check and medications, diabetic people require daily attention and care. Level-2 diabetes often requires regular intake of insulin. The solution proposed is to have a multi-platform environment in which we intend to build a personal assistant-based ecosystem that will help you to keep track of your health by tracking your body, namely, glucose, pressure, pulse and temperature, store data such as make appointments, view or inform booked appointments, keep track of prescription medication. The consolidated medical database that houses patient information includes vital information, referral records of medications, treatments, and prescriptions. The combination of the mobile app and wearable par allows user information to be gathered, such as vital information, drug intake events, appointment notifications, and medication intakes. Many health-care services also handle the medical status of the patient. Due to its ability to build hybrid applications that support both android and iOS with the same code base, React Native was selected. It also saved us a lot of time to introduce some of the existing features more common to the ecosystems of Android and iOS. Since the user's data is very sensitive, an organization should have access to information. Therefore, the health data exchanged should be encrypted for the safety of the user. In fact, the transmitted health data should be protected for the user's privacy. We need pull and push modes in which data is transmitted to the mobile app or into the Google server as such, as part of which Google fit applications hold the user fitness data.

4.2   INFRASTRUCTURE

These steps are used to export data to the Health App once QS Access is activated: by starting the QS Access for iPhone. To export, we choose rows and tap Create Table. Access to user information is then provided to the Health Kit; then we can pick 1 h and press all feasible rows. The Service Provider deploys service module in the U-healthcare infrastructure into the mobile system of the user when the user selects the services that the user wants to use. We plan to integrate with the pulse oximeter first as this software is designed specifically for patients with diabetes. We have not actively begun designing, but we have in-depth research and defined the criteria for selecting the type of device needed, as well as the Arduino boards and software configuration we need to incorporate the necessary hardware into the project. Since the mobile computing power of the user is very limited, only selected services are uploaded from the provider and installed in the user's portable device. Once purchased and mounted in the portable scheme, the service modules are controlled by the officer. The associated device descriptions and service suppliers will be downloaded to the user's mobile computer from the service supplier once the user begins switching on the Wearable Sensing Device. Thus, felt information can be assessed in the portable scheme using context-aware middleware. In the mobile system, the Context-Aware Middleware handles and analyzes sensed information and then produces sensed data for context. Caregiver can track the health information of the patient personally if clinical data is stored in the healthcare system. It is therefore essential to handle health data on the health-care system (Fig. 4.2).

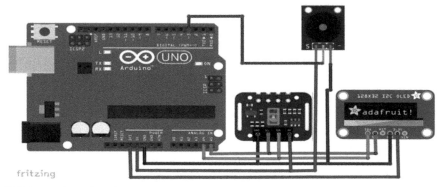

FIGURE 4.2   U-healthcare architecture.

4.3   CDSS AND WELLBEING-BASED HEALTHCARE SERVER

In U-healthcare infrastructure, the heath data is stored in the health-care server. Health-care server should therefore be a larger storage system for effective management of health data. Healthcare server also automatically analyzes health data and notifies user and caregiver of the analyzed result. We connected the Heart Beat Sensor with the Arduino where it contains of (three pin) connected the Pin (GND) to (GND) in Arduino and the Pin (VCC) to (5V) in Arduino and the Pin (S) to Pin (A0) in Arduino. Body Temperature Sensor consists of sensor contains of (four pin) which (GND, VCC, SCL, SDL), connected the Pin (GND) to (GND) in Arduino and the Pin (VCC) to Pin (5V) in Arduino and connected the Pin (VCC) to (Vout) in Voltage Step Down and Pin (GND) to Pin (GND) in Voltage Step Down and connected the Pin (GND) of Arduino to the (GND) in Voltage Step Down (for synchronization purpose). Generate the customer profile that includes user data and health threshold management and deployment. It displays the health condition of the user and the raw information depending on the power of access. The encrypted health information that is transmitted from the portable user scheme is decrypted and stored. Stored health information is analyzed using knowledge base such as CDSS or well-being. It automatically notifies the client and caregiver of the recorded information consequence.

When the diagnosis system passes this safety attribute value, the diagnosis system encrypts this information for data security (Table 4.1).

TABLE 4.1   Calculations Involving Action of Data and Clinical Psychologist.

Category	Contents	Category	Contents
	Name		Heart rate
	Height		SKT
	Weight		Respiration rate
	Age		Body fat rate
	Gender		BMI
	Phone number		Stress level
	Emergency contact		Glucose measure
	Phone number		Value
Attending physician	Physician ID		Blood pressure
	Physician major		Stress level
	Hospital information		Consumed calories

The current use of mental health devices for patients and clinicians (Zhou et al., 2016; Fleming et al., 2018; Noel et al., 2018; McNiel and Binder, 2018) remains low. This can be related to the pace of innovation that pushes virtual mental health beyond internal restrictions on medical devices, medical–legal standards (Hilty et al., 2018a, b; Torous et al., 2018), privacy laws (Glenn and Monteith, 2014), and even clinical evidence (Bhugra et al., 2017). This information is encrypted and then transmitted to the Healthcare Server's Monitoring Data Collector. Basal metabolic index for any individual is evaluated. This will be recorded online and a JSON file will be logged on. The Data Collect gathers raw data and stores these raw data to the Health Record Database (Fig. 4.3).

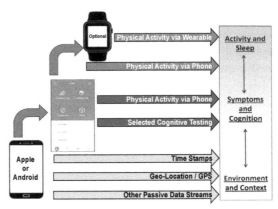

FIGURE 4.3   The process of remote monitoring service.

Health information shows related information from clients to text (or chart) for simple comprehension. When caregiver needs wellness information (or raw information) from the user, the caregiver regulates only access authority information appointed by the user. When the user clicks the medical server or alters user data using the User Interface, the User Profile Administrator generates or modifies the user profile by accessing the Medical file Server and then uses User Profile to Alert Development tools to classify the current situation (if the patient is in physiological emergency). The Context Aware Middleware evaluates the physiologically raw (user's) data that produces a health benefit. Then, to check emergency status, the data to the CDSS is passed as shown in Figure 4.4. The CDSS is used by context emergency management application for transfer

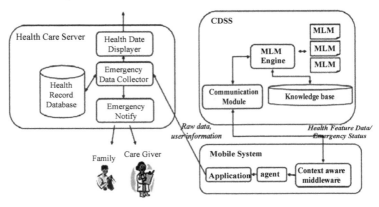

FIGURE 4.4   Identification of mobile system for data analysis.

of the user's raw data real timely as well as emergency previous file as shown in Figure 4.5. These raw data are sent to the Healthcare Server and authenticated. When the Healthcare Server receives an emergency file, the Emergency Notification Module must notify the status of the patient and user information, name, time of emergency, location of the user, and importance of the caregiver and family

4.4 IMPLEMENTATION OF THE MODEL

We built the U-healthcare infrastructure that consists of the mobile phone as a sensor device, wearable system, Healthcare Server, and CDSS in Figure 4.5.

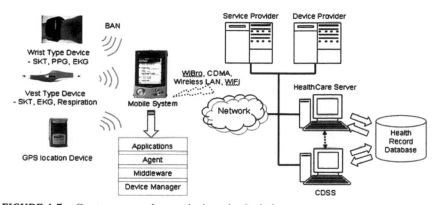

FIGURE 4.5   Context aware data analysis and calculation.

We have developed a shell of the health application, which is available on the Internet on this URL: https://tlukx.csb.app/. In this application, we used React.js to create an interface for the user.

This is used for identifying the systolic blood pressure.

In Figure 4.6, we show that the imported data is converted to the equivalent JSON file. Using the FETCH technique will be the most popular way to enter a JSON document in your React.js element. As all the data that we want is stored in an API, the fetch is how we ask for the information. We are basically implying, "Hey API, you can send me this data, here's what I want." Then the server will respond and be like, we created a straightforward contact list web page in this algorithm that presented contact information. We called a RESTful API and used React to display the browser response. We also addressed how the component DidMount() process works, how the state works, how components work, and how data can be collected from an API and data parsed to a component. The digital platform could also send real-time alerts to semi-specialized health-care providers, such as community health workers or other lay providers (Figs. 4.7 and 4.8).

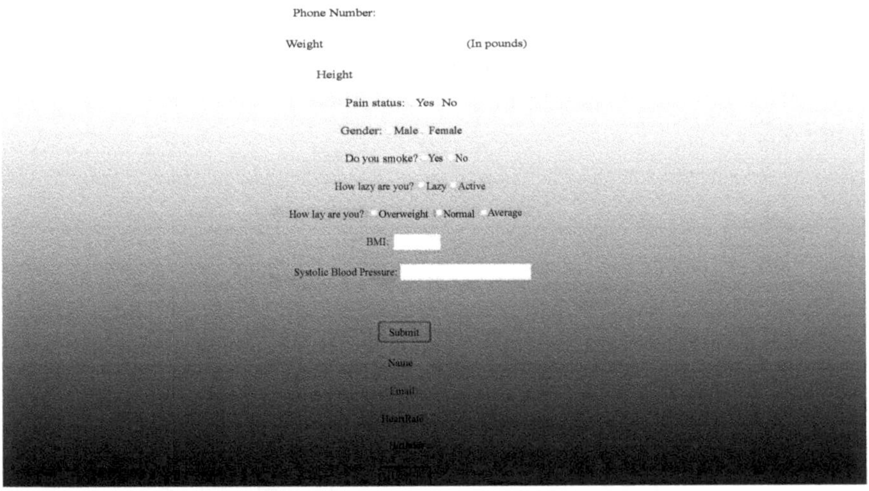

FIGURE 4.6   Flow diagram of the algorithm.

4.5   FUTURE WORK

In this chapter, for the management of health data, we have designed and developed CDSS and well-being healthcare server. Behavioral scientists suggest that without healthy psychological health, physical health won't be healthier. A successful mobile app can be an integrative system that will empower the user to improve his/her both physical and mental health. A provided technology's utility is measured not only by its reliability, but also by perceived ease of use, social support, and increased self-management. Mobile device captures and analyzes the user's clinical data in the U-health system. Mobile system also passes to the usable Healthcare Server the consumer health data and raw data. To do this, Healthcare Server must efficiently manage the health information of the user. Making mobile

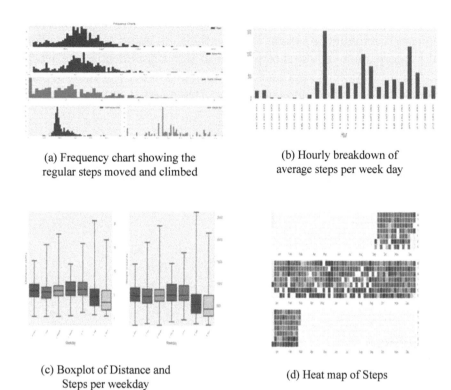

(a) Frequency chart showing the regular steps moved and climbed

(b) Hourly breakdown of average steps per week day

(c) Boxplot of Distance and Steps per weekday

(d) Heat map of Steps

FIGURE 4.7 Work related to heat map associated with distance and steps: (a) frequency chart showing the regular steps moved and climbed, (b) hourly breakdown of average steps per week day, (c) boxplot of distance and steps per weekday, (d) heat map of steps.

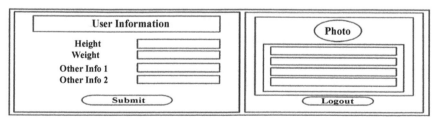

FIGURE 4.8 Implementation environment.

application user-friendly by integrating navigation and routing based on geo location, sharing habits, tips across their social network, and machine learning capabilities based on the medicine intake, habits, and activities, we can do pattern analysis and send this analysis to doctors so that they can share it across their patients to make their life better. Because patient health information and psychological profiling is confidential, we accept that data security technology and our healthcare system will automatically alert patients and clinicians about the reported medical and psychological information outcome.

KEYWORDS

- **health-care server**
- **health data**
- **well being**
- **perceived usefulness**
- **JSON**

REFERENCES

Bhugra, D.; Tasman, A.; Pathare, S.; Priebe, S.; Smith, S.; Torous, J., et al. The WPA-Lancet Psychiatry Commission on the Future of Psychiatry. *Lancet Psych.* **2017,** *4* (10), 775–818.

Di Matteo, D.; Fine, A.; Fotinos, K.; Rose, J.; Katzman, M. Patient Willingness to Consent to Mobile Phone Data Collection for Mental Health Apps: Structured Questionnaire. *JMIR Ment. Health* **2018,** *5* (3), e56.

Dowker, A. *Individual Differences in Arithmetic: Implications for Psychology, Neuroscience and Education*; Routledge: London, 2019.

Fleming, T.; Bavin, L.; Lucassen, M.; Stasiak, K.; Hopkins, S.; Merry, S. Beyond the Trial: Systematic Review of Real-world Uptake and Engagement with Digital Self-Help Interventions for Depression, Low Mood, or Anxiety. *J. Med. Internet Res.* **2018,** *20* (6), e199.

Gagnon, M. P.; Ngangue, P.; Payne-Gagnon, J.; Desmartis, M. m-Health Adoption by Healthcare Professionals: A Systematic Review. *J. Am. Med. Info. Assoc.* **2015,** *23* (1), 212–220.

Glenn, T.; Monteith, S. Privacy in the Digital World: Medical and Health Data Outside of HIPAA Protections. *Curr. Psychiatry Rep.* **2014,** *16* (11), 494.

Gong, J.; Anderson, F.; Fitzmaurice, G.; Grossman, T. In *Instrumenting and Analyzing Fabrication Activities, Users, and Expertise*, Proceedings of the 2019 CHI Conference on Human Factors in Computing Systems; ACM, April 2019; p 324.

Gulliver, A.; Banfield, M.; Morse, A. R.; Reynolds, J.; Miller, S.; Galati, C. A Peer-Led Electronic Mental Health Recovery App in a Community-Based Public Mental Health Service: Pilot Trial. *JMIR Form. Res.* **2019,** *3* (2), e12550.

Hilty, D. M.; Maheu, M. M.; Drude, K. P.; Hertlein, K. M. The Need to Implement and Evaluate Telehealth Competency Frameworks to Ensure Quality Care Across Behavioral Health Professions. *Acad. Psych.* **2018a,** *42* (6), 818–824.

Hilty, D. M.; Turvey, C.; Hwang, T. Lifelong Learning for Clinical Practice: How to Leverage Technology for Tele Behavioral Health Care and Digital Continuing Medical Education. *Curr. Psychiatry Rep.* **2018b,** *20* (3), 15.

Kirwan, M.; Vandelanotte, C.; Fenning, A.; Duncan, M. J. Diabetes Self-Management Smartphone Application for Adults with Type 1 Diabetes: Randomized Controlled Trial. *J. Med. Internet Res.* **2013,** *15*: e235; doi: 10.2196/jmir.2588.

Love-Koh, J.; Peel, A.; Rejon-Parrilla, J. C.; Ennis, K.; Lovett, R.; Manca, A.; … Taylor, M. The Future of Precision Medicine: Potential Impacts for Health Technology Assessment. *Pharmaco Eco.* **2018,** *36* (12), 1439–1451.

McNiel, D. E.; Binder, R. Current Regulation of Mobile Mental Health Applications. *J. Am. Acad. Psychiatry Law* **2018,** *46*, 204–211.

Noel, V. A.; Acquilano, S. C.; Carpenter-Song, E.; Drake, R. E. Assessing People with Serious Mental Illness' Use of Mobile and Computer Devices to Support Recovery. *JMIR Ment. Health* **2018**; https:// doi.org/10.2196/12255.

Nundy, S.; Mishra, A.; Hogan, P.; Lee, S. M.; Solomon, M. C.; Peek, M. E. How Do Mobile Phone Diabetes Programs Drive Behavior Change? Evidence from a Mixed Methods Observational Cohort Study. *Diab. Edu.* **2014,** *40*, 806–819; doi: 10.1177/0145721714551992.

Ruggiero, L.; Moadsiri, A.; Quinn, L. T.; Riley, B. B.; Danielson, K. K.; Monahan, C. et al. Diabetes Island: Preliminary Impact of a Virtual World Self-Care Educational Intervention for African Americans with Type 2 Diabetes. *JMIR Ser. Games* **2014,** *2*, e10; doi: 10.2196/games.3260.

Sarkar, U.; Gourley, G. I.; Lyles, C. R.; Tieu, L.; Clarity, C.; Newmark, L., et al. Usability of Commercially Available Mobile Applications for Diverse Patients. *J. Gen. Intern. Med.* **2016,** *31* (12), 1417–1426.

Torous, J.; Wisniewski, H.; Liu, G.; Keshavan, M. Mental Health Mobile Phone App Usage, Concerns, and Benefits Among Psychiatric Outpatients: Comparative Survey Study. *JMIR Ment. Health* **2018,** *5* (4).

Türk, E. Ç.; Altiner, E. P.; Özdemir, M.; Eroğul, O. In *Wireless Transmission of Heart Rate and Blood Pressure Measurements for Remote Patient Monitoring,* 2019 Medical Technologies Congress (TIPTEKNO); IEEE, Oct 2019; pp 1–4.

Wang, Y.; Kung, L.; Byrd, T. A. Big Data Analytics: Understanding Its Capabilities and Potential Benefits for Healthcare Organizations. *Technol. Forecast. Soc. Change* **2018,** *126*, 3–13.

Zhou, W.; Chen, M.; Yuan, J.; Sun, Y. W. A Smart Phone-Based Diabetes Management Application—Improves Blood Glucose Control in Chinese People with Diabetes. *Diab. Res. Clin. Pract.* **2016,** *116*, 105–110; doi: 10.1016/j.diabres.2016.03.018.

CHAPTER 5

Blockchain Technique-Based Smart Health Record System

JAYAPADMINI KANCHAN[1*], MADHURA N. HEGDE[1], ASHA B. SHETTY[1], RAJATHA[2], and K. GANARAJ[1]

[1]Information Science & Engineering Department, Sahyadri College of Engineering and Management Adyar, Mangaluru, India

[2]Information Science & Engineering Department, SJBIT, Bangalore, India

*Corresponding author. E-mail: jayapadmini@gmail.com

ABSTRACT

MedRecord focuses on storing medical records of patients in a decentralized network in order to provide security and privacy to the data of the patient. Smart contract is used to provide conflict-free service without the help of a third party. Smart contract is created in a platform called Ethereum. Hence, by using blockchain, we can safekeep and secure the medical reports of a patient.

5.1 INTRODUCTION

In today's world, all devices are interconnected to each other via networks. Various devices in homes, offices, cars, production plants, etc. perform various tasks to help with daily tasks. The number of connected devices keeps increasing all the time as manufactures present new internet-connected devices for helping the users in their day-to-day life, creating new digital experiences. IoT includes adding web availability to an arrangement of interrelated registering gadgets, mechanical and advanced machines, items, creatures, or potentially individuals. Every "thing" is given an interesting identifier and the capacity to exchange information over a system. Enabling gadgets to associate with the Web opens them up to various genuine vulnerabilities on the off chance that they are not appropriately secured.

Security and privacy are the key issues ever since the first two computers were connected to each other. With the commercialization of the internet security, concerns broadened to threats including hacking, phishing, eavesdropping, and attacks like DoS, DDoS, SQL injection, and man-in-the-middle attack.

From remotely monitoring a shrewd production line, to advantageously telecommuting, to unwinding in a driverless vehicle, the Internet of Things (IoT) is preparing for some energizing new chances. For organizations, IoT implies new ventures, new plans of action, and new income streams. Be that as it may, the innate idea of IoT—associating "things" to one another and to the cloud to frame a system—offers ascend to a large group of new security dangers. IoT is going to be the future of network of smart things, so it should be able to interconnect millions of smart objects to the Internet. Hence, there is a need for flexible architecture layers. As the applications vary in various walks of life, they have different architecture; hence, there is not a single architecture that can be termed as the model architecture. The architecture has three layers, namely, Hardware, Middleware, and Presentation layers. The Hardware layer consists of sensors, actuators, and embedded communication hardware; the Middleware has on-demand cloud storage and the computing tools. The Presentation layer has the easy-to-understand visualization. There are many architectures proposed for various applications, but basically it has three basic layers consisting of the Application, Network, and Perception layers. The architecture layers are as shown in Figure 5.1. In this system, same three-layer architecture is followed.

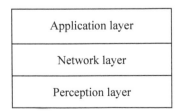

FIGURE 5.1   Architecture layers.

5.1.1   PERCEPTION LAYER

The first layer is the object or perception layer that uses a physical sensor to monitor the process and collect information. Actuators are also included in the object layer. Sensors such as temperature, humidity, accelerometer, weight, and motion are used to collect information. Here the information about the process is obtained in digital form and is further forwarded to the network layer through the channel securely. All the data in the system is generated in this layer.

5.1.2   NETWORK LAYER

This layer transfers the data created in the perception layer to the cloud. Various technologies are used to transfer the data, namely, 3G, GSM, Ethernet, Wi-Fi, Bluetooth, and ZigBee. The transfer of data is secured using these technologies. And the data is transferred using protocols such as HTTP and FTP. This layer also performs the process of cloud computing and data management.

It also manages the pairing of a service with its requester based on names and address. It enables the programmer to work with objects without knowing or considering the specific hardware platform. It also makes decision on the data received from the layers below it.

5.1.3   APPLICATION LAYER

This is the layer where the services are requested by the customers. As indicated by the applications, this layer gives the data to the clients, for example, the temperature and air mugginess readings, and so on. In this framework, it gives the ongoing information of stopping framework. This layer is most significant as it gives the exceptionally exact and immense arrangement of information in an efficient way. It keeps the user away from perplexity as it conveys the information in a problem-free way.

5.1.3.1   HOW DOES IOT WORK?

Gadgets and articles with inherent sensors are associated with an IoT stage, which coordinates information from different gadgets and afterward applies examination to gather the most significant data with applications to address explicit needs. IoT sensors see precisely which data is helpful and which ought to be overlooked. This data can be utilized to recognize designs, suggestive proposals, and distinguish potential issues before they happen.

A large portion of the system manages the utilization of remote sensor systems, gathers the information from different sorts of sensors, and afterward sends it to the principle server by means of remote convention. Accumulated information gives critical data about natural variables, which thusly screens the framework. Observing natural components is not the final answer for improving the yield as the efficiency is likewise influenced by different variables like assaults by creepy-crawlies, wild creatures, lack of harvests, and deficiency of water. So, in order to give answers for such issues, we need an incorporated framework that manages checking of outer factors as well as observing of the field information. The chapter clarifies the keen farming utilizing computerization and the highlights including a brilliant GPS-based remote detecting framework to perform assignments like weeding, showering, dampness detecting, sophisticated water system, and shrewd distribution center administration that incorporates temperature and moistness upkeep, robbery control, and so forth.

5.1.4   IOT SECURITY CHALLENGES

A number of challenges prevent the securing of IoT devices and ensuring end-to-end security in an IoT environment. Since systems administration machines and different items are moderately new, security has not generally been viewed as top need during an item's plan stage. Furthermore, in light of the fact that IoT is a beginning business sector, numerous item designers and makers are progressively keen on getting their items to showcase rapidly, as opposed to finding a way to fabricate security in from the beginning. A noteworthy issue referred to with IoT security is the utilization of hardcoded or default passwords, which can prompt security breaks. Regardless of whether passwords are transformed, they are regularly not sufficiently able to avert penetration.

Another basic issue confronting IoT gadgets is that they are frequently asset obliged and do not contain the process assets important to actualize solid security. All things considered, numerous gadgets do not or cannot offer propelled security highlights. For instance, sensors that screen dampness or temperature cannot deal with cutting-edge encryption or other safety efforts. Besides, the same number of IoT gadgets are "set it and overlook it"—set in the field or on a machine and left until part of the bargain—they barely ever get security updates or fixes. From a producer's perspective, building security in from the beginning can be expensive, hinder improvement, and cause the gadget not to work as it should. Interfacing heritage resources not intrinsically intended for IoT network is another security challenge. Supplanting heritage foundation with associated innovation is cost-restrictive, and such huge numbers of advantages will be retrofitted with brilliant sensors. In any case, as heritage resources that probably have not been refreshed or ever had protection from current dangers, the assault surface is extended. IoT security is likewise tormented by an absence of industry-acknowledged models. While numerous IoT security systems exist, there is no single settled upon structure. Enormous organizations and industry associations may have their very own particular norms, while certain sections, for example, modern IoT, have restrictive, inconsistent models from industry pioneers. The assortment of these gauges makes it hard to verify frameworks, yet in addition guarantee interoperability between them.

5.1.5 BUILDING SECURITY IN IOT FROM THE BOTTOM-UP

Security must be tended to all through the gadget lifecycle, from the underlying structure to the operational condition:

Secure booting: When power is first acquainted with the device, the realness and respectability of the product on the gadget is verified utilizing cryptographically created advanced signatures. Similarly as an individual signs a check or a legal document, a computerized mark appended to the product image and confirmed by the gadget guarantees that the lone product that has been approved to keep running on that gadget, and marked by the entity that approved it, will be stacked. The establishment of trust has been set up, yet the gadget still needs protection from different run-time dangers and malevolent expectations.

Access control: Next, various types of asset and access control are applied. Compulsory or job-based access controls built into the working framework limit the benefits of device components and applications, so they get to just the resources they need to carry out their responsibilities. In the event that any segment is compromised, access control guarantees that the gate rasher has as insignificant access to different pieces of the framework as could be allowed. Gadget-based access control instruments are similar to organize-based access control frameworks, for example, Microsoft Active Directory: even if somebody figures out how to take corporate certifications to gain access to a system, bargained data would be restricted to just those regions of the system approved by those specific qualifications. The standard of least benefit directs that the lone negligible access required to play out a capacity ought to be approved so as to limit the viability of any rupture of security.

Device validation: When the gadget is connected to the system, it ought to confirm itself before accepting or transmitting information. Profoundly implanted gadgets regularly do not have clients sitting behind consoles, holding on to enter the qualifications required to get to the system. How, at that point, would we be able to guarantee that those gadgets are distinguished effectively preceding approval? Similarly, as client confirmation enables a client to get to a corporate system dependent on client name and secret phrase, machine validation enables a gadget to get to a system dependent on a comparative arrangement of certifications put away in a protected stockpiling region.

Firewalling and IPS: The gadget additionally needs a firewall or profound parcel review capacity to control traffic that is bound to end at the gadget. For what reason is a host-based firewall or IPS required if organize-based apparatuses are set up? Profoundly inserted gadgets have one of a kind convention, unmistakable from big business IT conventions. For example, the brilliant vitality network has its very own arrangement of conventions administering how gadgets converse with one another. That is the reason business explicit convention separating and profound bundle review abilities are expected to distinguish malevolent payloads covering up in non-IT conventions. The gadget need not fret about sifting higher level, basic internet traffic—the system apparatuses should deal with that—yet it needs to channel the particular information bound to end on that gadget such that utilizes the restricted computational assets accessible.

Updates and fixes: Once the gadgets are in activity, it will begin getting hot patches and programming refreshes. Administrators need to take off patches, and gadgets need to verify them, in a way that does not expend data transfer capacity or debilitate the practical wellbeing of the gadget. It is one thing when Microsoft sends updates to Windows clients and ties up their workstations for 15 min. But it is another when a huge number of gadgets in the field are performing basic capacities or benefits and are reliant on security patches to ensure against the unavoidable powerlessness that breaks into nature. Programming updates and security patches must be conveyed, such that moderates the constrained data transfer capacity and discontinuous network of an installed gadget and completely dispenses with the plausibility of bargaining practical wellbeing.

5.1.6 THE END-TO-END SECURITY SOLUTION

Security at both the gadget and system levels is basic to the operation of IoT. A similar insight that empowers gadgets to perform their assignments should likewise empower them to perceive and counter act threats. Luckily, this does not require a revolutionary approach, yet rather a development of measures that have proven successful in IT systems, adjusted to the difficulties of IoT and to the limitations of associated gadgets. Rather than scanning for an answer that doesn't yet exist, or proposing a progressive way to deal with security, Wind River is concentrating on conveying the ebb and flow best-in-class IT security controls, streamlined for the new and very unpredictable installed applications driving the IoT.

Normal IoT safety efforts include,

- Incorporating security at the plan stage. IoT designers ought to incorporate security toward the beginning of any shopper, venture or modern-based gadget improvement. Empowering security naturally is basic, just as giving the latest working frameworks and utilizing secure equipment.
- Hardcoded certifications ought to never be a piece of the plan procedure. An extra measure engineers can take is to require qualifications be refreshed by a client before the gadget capacities. On the off chance that a gadget accompanies default accreditations, clients

should refresh them utilizing a solid secret phrase or multifaceted confirmation or biometrics where conceivable.

- Public key infrastructure (PKI) and digital certificates. PKI and 509 computerized declarations assume basic jobs in the improvement of secure IoT gadgets, giving the trust and control expected to disperse and recognize open encryption keys, secure information trades over systems, and check personality.

- Application execution marker (API) security. API security is basic to ensure the trustworthiness of information being sent from IoT gadgets to back-end frameworks and guarantee just approved gadgets, designers, and applications communicate with APIs.

- Identity management. Providing each device with a unique identifier is critical to understanding what the device is, how it behaves, the other devices it interacts with, and the proper security measures that should be taken for that device.

- Hardware security. Endpoint hardening includes making devices tamper-proof or tamper-evident. This is especially important when devices will be used in harsh environments or where they will not be monitored physically.

- Strong encryption is critical to securing communication between devices. Data at rest and in transit should be secured using cryptographic algorithms. This includes the use of key lifecycle management.

- Network security. Ensuring an IoT system incorporates guaranteeing port security, crippling port sending, and never opening ports when not required; utilizing antimalware, firewalls, and interruption location framework/interruption counteractive action framework; blocking unapproved IP addresses; and guaranteeing frameworks are fixed and state-of-the-art.

- Network access control (NAC). NAC can help identify and inventory IoT devices connecting to a network. This will provide a baseline for tracking and monitoring devices. IoT devices that need to connect directly to the Internet should be segmented into their own networks and have access to enterprise network restricted. Network segments should be monitoring for anomalous activity, where action can be taken, should an issue be detected.

- Security gateways. Going about as a middle person between IoT gadgets and the system, security portals have additionally handling force, memory, and capacities than the IoT gadgets themselves, which gives them the capacity to actualize highlights, for example, firewalls to guarantee programmers cannot get to the IoT gadgets they interface.

- Patch management/continuous software updates. Providing means of updating devices and software either over network connections or through automation is critical. Having a coordinated disclosure of vulnerabilities is also important to updating devices as soon as possible. Consider end-of-life strategies as well.
- IoT and operational system security are new to many existing security teams. It is critical to keep security staff up to date with new or unknown systems, learn new architectures and programming languages, and be ready for new security challenges. C-level and cybersecurity teams should receive regular training to keep up with modern threats and security measures.
- Integrating teams. Along with training, integrating disparate and regularly siloed teams can be useful. For example, having programing developers work with security specialists can help ensure the proper controls are added to devices during the development phase.
- Consumer education. Consumers must be made aware of the dangers of IoT systems and provided steps they can take to stay secure, such as updating default credentials and applying software updates. Consumers can also play a role in requiring device manufacturers to create secure devices and refusing to use those that do not meet high security standards.

Blockchain in a decentralized and distributed storage network for continuously growing record. Block consists of actual data and the hash of the previous block. Here, there are two types of blocks: user block and the file block.

User block contains the information of the users performing the transactions, and the file block consists of the information about the records uploaded by the user. Users can be doctor, patient, and anyone related with that domain. Doctor uploads the medical reports of his patient such as scanning report, X-ray report, or any other related reports of the patient. A patient who wants to access the data uploaded by the doctor have to enter the Aadhar card number of the doctor. They will get the list of files uploaded by the doctor. The patient cannot see the actual data, rather they can see the hash value of the file. They can request for the particular file based on the file description given by the doctor by clicking on ask permission. Once the patient clicks on ask permission, the doctor will get the notification regarding the request sent by the patient. The doctor can grant permission or can deny it. If the doctor grants permission, only then the patient can access the data by downloading it. Else patient cannot access the data without the permission of doctor. The data uploaded by the doctor is stored in the interplanetary file system (IPFS), and just the hash is stored in the blockchain. Once the permission is granted then they can download it from the IPFS.

5.1.7   ARCHITECTURE OF THE PROPOSED MODEL

The architecture diagram shows how the components of the system are related to each other. Figure 5.2 describes the architecture of the model. There are two types of users in this system: the Doctor and the Patient. Any user who wants to access the blockchain have to first register themselves using their Aadhar card number and login to the MedRecord.

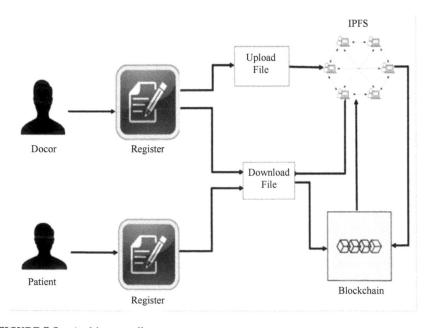

FIGURE 5.2   Architecture diagram.

Once the users are registered then they can upload the file. Doctor will upload the patient file to the blockchain. The actual file will be stored in the IPFS, but the hash of the location is stored in the new block. This new block is then verified by the users in the network and then added to the blockchain. Downloading of the file can be done by all the users only if they have the permission to access. To download the file, first they have to fetch the hash of the location from the block and then search for the file in that location in IPFS then download the actual file.

5.2 METHODOLOGY

Blockchain is a chain of blocks, where each block consists of actual data, hash of previous block, and timestamp. Hash of each block is produced based on the hash of the previous block. Thus, alteration of any block is not possible until the hash of the previous blocks is known. So, the data stored in the blocks remains secure. Once the block is created and added to blockchain, the blockchain cannot be tampered.

The sensitive information in patients' health records needs to be secure and protected. Blockchain provides a trustable and secure system to store health records of patients. In the distributed ledger of MedRecord, users include the doctors, patients, and family members. Two blockchains are created in the process. First is the user blockchain, which is the growing lists of blocks containing information about the users present in the distributed ledger. When a user registers himself to the MedRecord System, based on the user information a block is created and added to the blockchain. This way user data is stored and kept secure. Second is the file block, which contains information of the files uploaded by the users. This block contains the health records of the patients.

5.2.1 WORKING OF MEDRECORD

1. User registers through Aadhar number into MedRecord System.

   a. A block containing user information is created based on hash of previous block.
   b. The block is added to the user blockchain.

2. User uploads the necessary health records of the patient to MedRecord.

    a. The file will be stored in the IPFS.
    b. A block containing hash of IPFS location is created.
    c. Block is added to the file blockchain.
    d. User gives the essential permissions for the file block, only the users who have the permission can access the file.

3. Users who need the file can request the owner for the file.
4. The owner of the file can grant or reject the requests.
5. The requested user can then download the file from IPFS.

5.3   RESULT AND ANALYSIS

This system results in safekeeping of the patient data. Once the report in uploaded, it is not directly shown to the users. The uploaded report is directly stored in IPFS, and the hash of the location is stored in the new block. Once the block is verified by the nodes in the network then it is added to the blockchain. Hence, no other user can access the data uploaded by the doctor without the actual permission. Since there is no third party involved and each block contains the previous block hash, value altering and damaging of the data is not possible.

FIGURE 5.3 Blocks in blockchain.

Every block contains the hash value, author information, date of upload, file size, title of the uploaded file, and description of the file content. Figure 5.3 shows the blocks present in the blockchain.

5.4   CONCLUSION AND FUTURE WORK

The proposed system allows the access of personal data of the patient to the authorized and permitted users. That is, the patient can be the owner of their own data and decide who can access to their data. Hence, it provides efficiency to the medical field as a whole.

KEYWORDS

- **blockchain**
- **smart contract**
- **Ethereum**
- **interplanetary file system**
- **distributed ledger**
- **mining**

REFERENCES

Aste, T.; Tasca, P.; Di Matteo, T. Blockchain Technologies: The Foreseeable Impact on Society and Industry. *IEEE Comput.* **2017,** *50* (9), 18–28.

Dinh, T. T. A.; Liu, R.; Zhang, M,; Chen, G.; Ooi, B. C.; Wang, J. Untangling Blockchain: A Data Processing View of Blockchain Systems. *IEEE Trans. Knowledge Data Eng.* **2018,** *30.* (7), 1366–1385.

Esposito, C.; De Santis, A.; Tortora, G.; Chang, H.; Raymond Choo, K.-K. Blockchain: A Panacea for Healthcare Cloud-Based Data Security and Privacy. *IEEE Cloud Comput.* **2018,** *5* (1), 31–37.

Hegadekatti, V.; Hegadekatti, K. Blockchain Technology and the Medical Sciences. *Int. J. Sci. Res.* **2018,** *7* (3).

Henry, R.; Herzberg, A.; Kate, A. Blockchain Access Privacy: Challenges and Directions. *IEEE Security Privacy* **2018,** *16* (4), 38–45.

Hoy, M. B. An Introduction to the Blockchain and Its Implications for Libraries and Medicine. *Taylor & Francis Med. Ref. Services Quar.* **2017,** *36* (3), 273–279.

Kshetri, N.; Voas, J.-R. Blockchain-enabled E-voting. *IEEE Softw.* **2018,** *35* (4), 95–99.

Kshetri, N.; Voas, J.-R. Blockchain in Developing Countries. *IEEE IT Prof.* **2018,** *20* (2), 11–14.

Kuo, T.-T.; Kim, H.-E.; Ohno-Machado, L. Blockchain Distributed Ledger Technologies for Biomedical and Healthcare Applications. *Ox. Univ. Press J. Am. Med. Inf. Assoc.* **2017,** *24* (6), 1211–1220.

Zhaofeng, M.; Weihua, H.; Wei, B.; Hongmin, G.; Zhen, W. A Master-Slave Blockchain Paradigm and Application in Digital Rights Management. *IEEE China Commun.* **2018,** *15* (8), 174–188.

CHAPTER 6

Security Issues and Challenges in the Internet of Things (IoT)

MADHURA N. HEGDE*, JAYAPADMINI KANCHAN, ASHA B. SHETTY,
D. R. JANARDHANA, and K. GANARAJ

*Information Science and Engineering Department, Sahyadri College of
Engineering and Management, Adyar, Mangalore, Karnataka, India*

Corresponding author. E-mail: madhuhegede@gmail.com

ABSTRACT

Remote correspondence frameworks are exceedingly disposed to security
perils. The critical usages of remote correspondence frameworks are in
military, business, human administrations, retail, and transportations.
These structures use wired, cell, or ad hoc frameworks. Remote sensor
frameworks, actuator frameworks, and vehicular frameworks have gotten
a fantastic thought in the open eye and industry. Of late, the Internet of
things (IoT) has become broad research thought. The IoT is considered
as possible destiny of the Web. In future, IoT will accept a vital activity
and change our living styles, standards, similarly to game plans. The use
of IoT in different applications is required to rise rapidly in the coming
years. The IoT grants billions of devices, society, and organizations to
connect with others and exchange information. Due to the extended usage
of IoT contraptions, the IoT frameworks are slanted to various security
strikes. The presence of successful security and assurance shows that IoT
frameworks are incredibly expected to ensure protection, get the chance to
control, and decency, among others. In this chapter, a complete assessment
on security and insurance issues in IoT frameworks is provided.

6.1   INTRODUCTION

Internet of things (IoT) has gained   significant attention during the previous couple of years. The idea of IoT was initially proposed by Kevin Ashton in 1999. Because of quick headways in versatile correspondence, wireless sensor networks, radio frequency identification (RFID), and distributed computing, interchanges among IoT gadgets have turned out to be more advantageous than it was previously. IoT gadgets are equipped for coworking with each other. The world of IoT incorporates a gigantic assortment of gadgets such as advanced mobile phones, PCs, PDAs, workstations, tablets, and other handheld implanted gadgets. The IoT gadgets depend on savvy sensors and remote correspondence frameworks to speak with one another and move important data to the unified framework. The data from IoT gadgets is additionally handled in the unified framework and conveyed to the proposed goals. With the quick development of correspondence and web innovation, our everyday schedules are increasingly focused on an anecdotal space of virtual world.[1] Individuals can work, shop, visit (keep pets and plants in the virtual world given by the system), though people live in reality. Hence, it is exceptionally hard to supplant all the human exercises with the completely robotized living. There is a jumping point of confinement of anecdotal space that limits the future advancement of Web for better benefits. The IoT has effectively coordinated the anecdotal space and this presents reality on a similar stage. The significant focuses of IoT are simply the setup of a shrewd situation and hesitant autonomous gadgets, for example, brilliant living, keen things, savvy well-being, and shrewd urban areas.[2] Nowadays, the selection pace of the IoT gadgets is extremely high, and an ever-increasing number of gadgets are associated by means of the Web. As indicated by evaluation,[3] there are 30 billion associated things with rough 200 billion associations that will create income of around 700 billion euros continuously 2020. Presently in China, there are 9 billion gadgets that are required to arrive at 24 billion constantly 2020. In future, the IoT will totally change our living styles and plans of action. It will allow individuals and gadgets to convey whenever, wherever, with any gadget under perfect conditions utilizing any system and any administration.[4] The principle objective of IoT is to make a superior world for individuals in future.

Security and protection are the key issues as far back as the initial two PCs were associated with one another. With the commercialization of the web security, concerns expanded to dangers, including hacking, phishing, listening stealthily, and assaults like denial of service (DoS), distributed DoS (DDoS), SQL infusion, and man-in-the-center assault. From remotely monitoring a brilliant manufacturing plant, to helpfully telecommuting, to unwinding in a driverless vehicle, the IoT is preparing for some energizing new chances. For organizations, IoT implies new ventures, new plans of action, and new income streams. Be that as it may, the inborn idea of IoT—associating "things" to one another and to the cloud to frame a system—offers ascend to a large group of new security dangers.

IoT is going to be the future of network of smart things, so it should be able to interconnect millions of smart objects to the Internet. Hence there is a need for flexible architecture layers.

As the applications vary in various walks of life, they have different architecture, hence there is not a single architecture termed as model architecture. The architecture has three layers, hardware, middleware, and presentation layer. The hardware layer consists of sensors, actuators, and embedded communication hardware; the middleware has on-demand cloud storage and the computing tools; and the presentation layer has the easy to understand visualization.

There is much architecture proposed for various applications, but basically, it has three basic layers that are application, network, and perception layers. The architecture layers are shown in Figure 6.1. In this system, the three-layer architecture is followed.

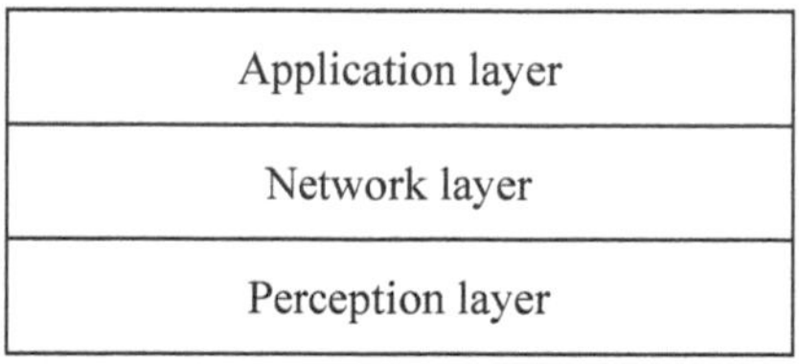

| Application layer |
| Network layer |
| Perception layer |

FIGURE 6.1   Architecture layers.

6.1.1   PERCEPTION LAYER

The first component of IoT is the object or perception layer, and it uses a physical sensor to monitor the process and collect information. Actuators are also included in the object layer. Sensors such as temperature, humidity, accelerometer, weight, and motion are used to collect information. Here the information about the process is obtained in digital form and is further forwarded to the network layer through the channel securely. All the data in the system is generated in this layer.

6.1.2   NETWORK LAYER

This layer transfers the data created in the perception layer to the cloud. Various technologies are used to transfer the data, namely, 3G, GSM, Ethernet, Wi-Fi, Bluetooth, and ZigBee. The transfer of data is secured using these technologies. And the data is transferred using protocols such as HTTP and FTP. This layer also performs the process of cloud computing and data management.

It also manages the pairing of a service with its requester based on names and address. It enables the programmer to work with objects without knowing or considering the specific hardware platform. It also makes decision on the data received from the layers below it.

6.1.3   APPLICATION LAYER

This is the layer where the services are requested by the customers. According to the applications, this layer provides the information to the customers such as the temperature and air humidity readings. In this system, it provides the real-time data of parking system. This layer is most important as it provides the highly precise and vast set of data in a systematic manner. It avoids confusion as it represents the data in a hassle-free manner.

6.2   IOT APPLICATIONS

The main objectives of IoT are the configuration of a smart environment and self-conscious independent devices such as smart living, smart items, smart health, and smart cities.[2] The applications of IoT in industries, medical field, and in-home automation are discussed in the following sections.

6.2.1   IOT IN INDUSTRIES

The IoT has given a reasonable chance to manufacture huge modern frameworks and applications.[6] In a savvy IoT transportation framework, the approved individual can screen the current area and development of a vehicle. The approved individual can likewise anticipate its future area and street traffic. In the prior stage, the term "IoT" was utilized to distinguish one of a kind item with RFID. Hitherto, the specialists relate the term "IoT" with sensors, global positioning system gadgets, cell phones, and actuators. The acknowledgment and administrations of new IoT advancements primarily rely on the protection of information and security of data. The IoT grants numerous things to be associated, followed, and observed so important data and private information gathered consequently. In IoT condition, the security assurance is a progressively basic issue when contrasted with customary systems since quantities of assaults on IoT are high.

6.2.2   IOT IN PERSONAL MEDICAL DEVICES

The IoT gadgets are likewise generally utilized in social insurance frameworks for observing and appraisal of patients.[7] To screen the ailment of a patient, personal medical devices (PMDs) are either planted in patients' body or it might connect to patients' body remotely. PMDs are little electronic gadgets that are ending up exceptionally normal and prevalent. The market estimation of these gadgets is anticipated to associate with 17 billion USD by 2019.[8] These gadgets utilize a remote interface to perform correspondence with a base station that is additionally used to peruse status of the gadget, therapeutic reports, change parameters of the gadget, or update status on the gadget. Remote interface causes a great deal of security and protection dangers for the patient. The remote interface of such gadgets is anything but difficult to digital assaults that may endanger the patient's security, protection, and well-being. On account of medicinal services, the essential objective is to guarantee the security of system so as to keep the protection of patient from pernicious assaults. At the point when assailants assault cell phones, they have their predefined objectives. Typically, their point is to take the data, assault on gadgets to use their assets, or may close down certain applications that are checking patient's condition. There are numerous sorts of assaults on medical gadgets such as snooping that incorporates listening stealthily to the data in which security of the patient is compromised, inaccuracy in the medical reports that can be modified to undermine the gadgets' efficacy, and other accessibility attacks that deplete the battery and render the device inoperative . Some advanced security risks related to security, assurance, and prosperity of remedial data of patient are inspected as follows:

1. PMDs are basic to any errand that utilizations battery control. Thus, these gadgets must help a constrained encryption. In the event that the gadget is a piece of various systems, at that point, secrecy, accessibility, security, and trustworthiness will be at high chance.

2. As PMDs have no validation instrument for remote correspondence, so, the data put away in the gadget might be effectively gotten to by unapproved people.

3. The absence of secure validation additionally reveals the gadgets to numerous other security dangers that may prompt vindictive assaults. An antagonistic may dispatch DoS assaults.

4. The information of patient is sent over a transmission medium that might be adjusted by unapproved parties, and thus, security of a patient may be compromised.

6.2.3   IOT IN SMART HOME

The IoT brilliant home administrations are expanding step by step.[9] Advanced gadgets can adequately speak to one another utilizing Internet Protocol addresses. All savvy home gadgets are associated with the Web in a keen home condition. As the quantity of gadgets increases in the shrewd home condition, the odds of pernicious assaults likewise increase. In the event that savvy home gadgets are worked autonomously, the odds of vindictive assaults likewise diminish. By and by keen home gadgets can be gotten to through the Web wherever, whenever. In this way, it builds the odds of malignant assaults on these gadgets. A keen home comprises four sections: administration stage, brilliant gadgets, home door, and home system. In the brilliant home, numerous gadgets are associated and cleverly share data utilizing a home system. Therefore, there exists a home portal that controls the progression of data among keen gadgets associated with the outside system. Administration stage utilizes the administrations of specialist coop that convey various administrations to the home system.

6.3   SECURITY REQUIREMENTS

In IoT, each one of the gadgets and individuals is associated with one another to give administrations whenever and wherever. The greater part of the gadgets associated with the Web are not furnished with effective security components and are powerless against different protection and security issues, for example, secrecy, trustworthiness, and genuineness. For the IoT, some security prerequisites must be satisfied to keep the system from pernicious assaults.[7,10] Here, the absolute most required capacities of a safe system are quickly talked about.

Strength to assaults: The framework should be competent enough to recoup itself on the off-chance that it crashes during information transmission. For a model server working in a multiuser domain, it must be shrewd and sufficiently able to shield itself from gatecrashers or a busybody. On the off-chance that it is down, it would recuperate itself without implication to the clients of its down status.

Information authentication: The information and the related data must be validated. A validation system is utilized to permit information transmission from just real gadgets.

Access control: Only approved people are given access control. The framework manager must control access to the clients by dealing with their usernames and passwords and by characterizing their entrance rights, so that various clients can get to just a pertinent segment of the database or projects.

Customer security: The information and data ought to be in safe hands. Individual information should just be gotten to be approved individual to keep up the customer protection. It implies that no insignificant confirmed client from the framework or some other kind of customer can approach the private data of the customer.

6.3.1   IOT SECURITY, PRIVACY, THREATS, AND CHALLENGES

The age of IoT has changed our living styles. Although the IoT gives colossal advantages, it is inclined to different security dangers in our everyday life. Most of the security dangers are identified with spillage of data and loss of administrations. In IoT, the security dangers clearly are influencing the physical security chance. The IoT comprises various gadgets and stage with various qualifications, where each framework needs the security necessity relying on its attributes. The protection of a client is additionally the most significant part in light of the fact that a ton of individual data is being shared among different sorts. Dangers in tech savvy homes using IoT in household gadgets are numerous. Henceforth a safe system is expected to ensure the individual data. In addition to IoT administrations, there are various kinds of gadgets that perform correspondence utilizing various systems. It implies that there are a great deal of security issues on client protection and system layer. Client protection can likewise be revealed from various courses. Some security dangers in the IoT are as per the following:

1. E2E data life cycle insurance:

    To guarantee the security of information in IoT condition, start-to-finish information assurance is given in a total system. Information is gathered from various gadgets associated with one another and quickly imparted to different gadgets. Along these lines, it requires a structure to secure the information, classification of information and oversee data protection in full information life cycle.

2. Secure thing arranging:

    The interconnection and correspondence among the gadgets in the IoT change as indicated by the circumstance. Subsequently, the gadgets must be fit for keeping up security level. For instance, when nearby gadgets and sensors utilized in the locally situated system speak with one another securely, their correspondence with outside gadgets ought to likewise deal the with same security strategy.

3. Visible/usable security and protection:

    Most of the security and security concerns are conjured by misconfiguration of clients. It is extremely troublesome and unreasonable for clients to execute such protection approaches and complex security instrument. It is needed to select security and privacy policies that may apply automatically.

6.3.1.1 SECURITY THREATS IN SMART HOME

Keen home administrations can be presented to digital assaults since larger part of the specialist organization do not consider security parameters at the beginning. The conceivable security dangers in a shrewd home are listening stealthily, DDoS assaults and spillage of data, and so forth. Shrewd home systems are compromised by unapproved access. The conceivable security dangers to keen home are examined as pursues.

1. Trespass: If the shrewd entryway lock is affected by vindictive codes or it is gotten to by an unapproved party, the assailant can trespass on savvy home without crushing the entryway. The consequence of this impact could be a death toll or property. To dispose of such assaults, passwords ought to be changed as often as possible that must contain in any at least 10 characters as it is extremely hard for assailants to break a long secret key. Correspondingly, confirmation component and access control may likewise be connected.

2. Monitoring and individual data spillage: Safety is one of the significant motivations behind a keen home. Subsequently, there are a great deal of sensors that are utilized for flame checking, infant observing, housebreaking, and so on. On the off-chance that these sensors are hacked by an interloper, at that point, he can screen the home and access individual data. To keep away from this assault, information encryption must be connected among portals and sensors or client validation for the recognition of unapproved gatherings might be connected.

3. DoS/DDoS: Attackers may get to the savvy home system and send mass messages to shrewd gadgets, for example, clear to send/ request to send. They can likewise assault focused on gadget by utilizing malignant codes so as to perform DoS assaults on different gadgets that are associated in a brilliant home. Subsequently, keen gadgets cannot perform appropriate functionalities due to depleting assets because of such assaults. For evasion from this assault, it is essential to apply validation to square and recognize unapproved access.

4. Falsification: When the gadgets in shrewd home perform correspondence with the application server, the aggressor may gather the parcels by changing directing table in the portal. In spite of the

fact that the SSL (secure attachment layer) system is connected, an aggressor can sidestep the produced endorsement. Along these lines, the assailant can misconstrue the substance of information or may release the privacy of information. To verify the shrewd home system from this assault, SSL strategy with appropriate validation instrument ought to be connected. It is likewise imperative to square unapproved gadgets that may attempt to access shrewd home system.

The IoT is an idea that portrays future where the physical items associated with Web speak with one another and recognize themselves for different gadgets.[15] The IoT framework comprises brilliant items, cell phones, tablets, smart gadgets, and so forth. Such frameworks use RFID, quick response codes, or remote innovation to perform correspondence between various gadgets. The IoT fabricated associations from human-to-human, human-to-physical articles, and physical-to-other physical items. According to examination from IDC, there will be 30 billion web-associated gadgets by 2020. This fast development of web information needs progressively profitable and secure system.

6.3.1.2   IOT CHALLENGES

The security concern is the biggest challenge in IoT. The application data of IoT could be industrial, enterprise, consumer, or personal. This application data should be secured and must remain confidential against theft and tampering. For example, the IoT applications may store the results of a patient's health or shopping store. The IoT improves the correspondence between gadgets yet at the same time, there are issues identified with the versatility, accessibility, and reaction time. Security is where the information is safely transmitted over the Web. While moving the information crosswise over universal fringe, well-being measure act might be applied by government guideline, for example, Health Insurance Portability and Accountability Act. Among various security challenges, the most significant moves pertinent to IoT are discussed.

1. Information privacy: Some producers of brilliant TVs gather information about their clients to break down their survey propensities

so the information gathered by the savvy TVs may have a test for information security during transmission.

2. Data security: Data security is additionally an incredible test. While transmitting information flawlessly, it is critical to avoid watching gadgets on the Web.

3. Insurance concerns: The insurance agencies introducing IoT gadgets on vehicles gather information about well-being and driving status so as to take choices about protection.

4. Lack of common standard: Since there are numerous norms for IoT gadgets and IoT-producing ventures, it is a major test to recognize allowed and nonallowed gadgets associated with the Web.

5. Technical concerns: Due to the increased usage of IoT devices, the traffic generated by these devices is also increasing. Hence there is a need to increase network capacity; therefore, it is also a challenge to store the huge amount of data for analysis and further final storage.

6. Security attacks and system vulnerabilities: There has been a lot of work done in the scenario of IoT security up till now. The related work can be divided into system security, application security, and network security.[17]

    a. System security: System security mainly focuses on overall IoT system to identify different security challenges, to design different security frameworks, and to provide proper security guidelines in order to maintain the security of a network.

    b. Application security: Application security works for IoT application to handle security issues according to scenario requirements.

    c. Network security: Network security deals with securing the IoT communication network for communication of different IoT devices.

In the next section, the security concerns regarding IoT are discussed. The security attacks are categorized into four broad classes.

6.4   ANALYSIS OF DIFFERENT TYPES OF ATTACKS AND POSSIBLE SOLUTIONS

The IoT is facing various types of attacks, including active attacks and passive attacks that may easily disturb the functionality and abolish the benefits of its services. In a passive attack, an intruder just senses the node or may steal the information but never attacks physically. However, the active attacks disturb the performance physically. These dynamic assaults are arranged into two further classifications that are interior assaults and outside assaults. Such defenseless assaults can avert the gadgets to impart intelligently. Consequently, the security requirements must be applied to keep gadgets from noxious assaults. Various kinds of assault, nature/ conduct of assault, and risk level of assaults are talked about in this area. Various degrees of assaults are sorted into four kinds as indicated by their conduct and propose potential answers for dangers/assaults.

Low-level attack: If an attacker tries to attack a network and his attack is not successful.

1. Medium-level assault: If an aggressor/gatecrasher or a spy is simply tuning in to the medium yet do not modify the uprightness of information.

    High-level assault: If an assault is carried on a system and it changes the trustworthiness of information or alters the information.

2. Extremely high-level assault: If an interloper/assailant assaults on a system by increasing unapproved access and playing out an illicit activity, making the system inaccessible, sending mass messages, or sticking system.

6.5 CONCLUSION

The primary accentuation of this chapter was to feature real security issues of IoT, especially centering the security assaults and their countermeasures. Because of the absence of security features in gadgets using IoT, these have become easy prey to cyber crimes without the knowledge of the users which is unfortunate. In this chapter, the security prerequisites are examined, for example, privacy, uprightness, and confirmation. In this study, 12 distinct kinds of assaults are arranged as low-level, medium-level, abnormal-state, and incredibly abnormal-state assaults alongside their inclination/conduct just as recommended answers for experience these assaults are examined.

Considering the significance of security in IoT applications, it is extremely essential to introduce security system in IoT gadgets and correspondence systems. Besides, to shield from any interlopers or security risk, it is additionally prescribed not to utilize default passwords for the gadgets and read the security prerequisites for the gadgets before utilizing it them. Crippling the highlights that are not utilized may diminish the odds of security assaults. In addition, it is critical to think about various security conventions utilized in IoT gadgets and systems.

KEYWORDS

- **Internet of things**
- **security issues in IoT**
- **security**
- **privacy**

REFERENCES

1. Kumar, J. S.; Patel, D. R. A Survey on Internet of Things: Security and Privacy Issues. *Int. J. Comput. Appl.* **2014,** *90* (11).
2. Abomhara, M.; Køien, G. M. In *Security and Privacy in the Internet of Things: Current Status and Open Issues.* Privacy and Security in Mobile Systems (PRISMS), International Conference on; IEEE, 2014; pp 1–8.
3. Chen, S.; Xu, H.; Liu, D.; Hu, B.; Wang, H. A Vision of IoT: Applications, Challenges, and Opportunities with China Perspective. *IEEE IoT J.* **2014,** 1 (4), 349–359.
4. Atzori, L.; Iera, A.; Morabito, G. The Internet of Things: A Survey. *Comput. Netw.* **2010,** *54* (15), 2787–2805.
5. Hossain, M. M.; Fotouhi, M.; Hasan, R. In *Towards an Analysis of Security Issues, Challenges, and Open Problems in the Internet of Things.* Services (SERVICES), 2015 IEEE World Congress on; IEEE, 2015; pp 21–28.
6. Da Xu, L.; He, W.; Li, S. Internet of Things in Industries: A Survey. *IEEE Trans. Ind. Inform.* **2014,** *10* (4), 2233–2243.
7. Tarouco, L. M. R.; Bertholdo, L. M.; Granville, L. Z.; Arbiza, L. M. R.; Carbone, F.; Marotta, M.; de Santanna, J. J. C. In *Internet of Things in Healthcare: Interoperability and Security Issues.* Communications (ICC), IEEE International Conference on; IEEE, 2012; pp 6121–6125.
8. Mohan, A. In *Cyber Security for Personal Medical Devices Internet of Things.* Distributed Computing in Sensor Systems (DCOSS), 2014 IEEE International Conference on; IEEE, 2014; pp 372–374.
9. Yoon, S.; Park, H.; Yoo, H. S. Security Issues on Smart Home in IoT Environment. In *Computer Science and its Applications*; Springer, 2015; pp 691–696.

10. Weber, R. H. Internet of Things—New Security and Privacy Challenges. *Comput. Law Secur. Rev.* **2010,** *26* (1), 23–30.

CHAPTER 7

Demand of Internet Services in Infrastructure-as-a-Service (IaaS) to IoT-Cloud Application Move

SUDIP SIHA[1*], ANIRBAN DAS[2], and AMITAV GHOSH[3]

[1]*Seacom Skills University, West Bengal, India*

[2]*Department of Computer Science, University of Engineering and Management, Kolkata, India*

[3]*School of Management Studies, Seacom Skills University, West Bengal, India*

Corresponding author. E-mail: sudipepi@gmail.com

ABSTRACT

The key focus of enterprise organizations that operate globally is to provide better engagement with their customers, partner to enhance the quality of service in their supply chain, and add value to customer's business by solving their existing issues or helping them to grow through creativity, innovation, and more market penetration. To achieve the preceding points, new requirement in digitalization era and to save cost, customers are moving their on-premises applications into cloud services. Wide area network (WAN) will play pivotal role to support the application shift, and countries are realigning their WAN service strategy from conventional MPLS to internet-based VPN solution to get best fit for the purpose of infrastructure development. The scope of the current study is to analyze growth of internet-based WAN solution in last 5 years compared to MPLS service to strengthen digital footprint and easy access of cloud applications by local breakout to the public Internet through secured cloud proxy.

7.1   INTRODUCTION

Cloud service has been widely accepted by the industry since it has got features like faster deployment, easy scalability, on demand expansion or shortening of infrastructure, lesser local infrastructure/administrative overhead, managed service portfolio with security compliance, anywhere anytime secured access from any device including Internet of Things (IoT). In the virtual office/collaboration space, cloud applications are beneficial than on-premises hosting services, and internet-based VPN wide area network (WAN) solution with secure local internet breakout via cloud proxy is on rapid demanding.

Cloud can be private—not connected to public Internet, public—exposed to the Internet, or hybrid—dual home environment—one portion connected to private environment while another portion is connected to public environment.

Compared to private cloud environment, demand of public cloud is increasing rapidly as cloud service providers are meeting industry best practices and security standard for audit compliance. Enterprise organizations are looking for closed proximity of internet cloud–based application access for better cloud application response, which is the key driver of moving from MPLS to internet-based VPN solution where either split tunnel or cloud proxy–based local internet breakout mechanism has been adapted as standard approach.

Split tunnel means creating two tunnels in the VPN router, one is trusted tunnel for intranet application access for the organization, and the other tunnel is direct internet access that gives faster access for internet applications. But security may be a major concern for the organization as direct internet access will lead security vulnerability with wide span of threat landscape. Direct internet access will not give any URL filtering or content-blocking feature, and if any computer is infected, it can propagate across the organization. To overcome the security challenge, cloud proxy–based solution has been evolved where VPN router can have two tunnels, one private for intranet application access and the other connected to cloud proxy solution where default route is blocked in the firewall rule, and URL blocking and content filtering feature is there for organization to define their security policy based on their compliance requirement. This approach is widely accepted in pre-software-defined WAN (SD-WAN) phase.

For dual-MPLS site or single-MPLS site, internet breakout is not local, and they have to go via MPLS backbone to use network-based firewall (NBFW), which is a gateway from MPLS to the public Internet for accessing publicly hosted internet applications or web browsing. For private/public cloud-based application access, express route may be another approach to securely access cloud-based applications via MPLS and cloud service–provided gateway. The key challenge is that if express route or NBFW is not in the region, latency to access cloud-specific application or web browsing will be higher compared to local internet breakout.

The current study will focus on how in last 5 years internet-based VPN and cloud proxy solution has been evolved in different regions (Fig. 7.1).

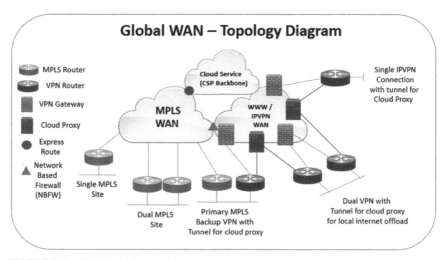

FIGURE 7.1   WAN architecture for enterprise network.

7.2   LITERATURE REVIEW

Internet World Stats published a report[1,5] in their website in April 2019 regarding the growth of the Internet compared to percentage of population since December 1995 to Q1 2019, which shows huge growth from 0.4 to 56%, and in last 5 years, it is around 10%, which is relatively inspiring.

The Next Web published an article[2,6] in March 2017, regarding growth of the Internet per geographic region in last 5 years, and growth was highlighted due to social media penetration, but growth of internet enterprise customer was not highlighted.

McKinsey published an article in October 2011 by James Manyika and Charles Roxburgh[3,7] which focused on the impact of the Internet on economic growth and prosperity, mapping the GDP rise in last 5 years of internet technology revolution. Security risks were highlighted to combat future challenges, but how enterprise segment is aligned with this growth was not highlighted.

Forbes report published in May 2018 by Bernard Marr highlighted that the volume of data is being generated with growth of public internet connectivity, but how enterprise customers are aligned was not discussed in detail.

Statista published a review paper in December 2018 regarding the number of internet users worldwide from 2005 to 2018 (in millions),[4,5] which shows potential growth of 2.1 M to 3.8k M, which is considerably high but the growth of enterprise was missing.

The Best VPN published a statistical analysis in March 2019 by John Mason[10] related to VPN statistics and usage, but it only focused on site to client VPN, site to site VPN, and related growth for the enterprise organization was not focused.

VPN Mentor published an article in April 2019[11] to present statistical analysis of end users' growth in VPN connectivity. Office-to-office communication was not highlighted.

VPN Mentor published a review paper in April 2019[12] on country-specific trends, highlighting Internet Trends 2019. Stats & Facts in the United States and worldwide is more end user specific rather than interoffice communication in the corporate segment.

Growth of cloud proxy service for internet offloading for enterprise organizations was not highlighted in the statistical report.

7.3   OBJECTIVE

The objective of the current study is to analyze growth of internet-based VPN service (site-to-site VPN) for the enterprise organization across the globe and growth of cloud proxy service for internet browsing offload in last 5 years. The study will focus on finding answers of the following questions to have visibility of trend for enterprise organization for adapting internet-based technology for their WAN service delivery as part of cloud application move compared to MPLS solution.

- What is the worldwide growth percentage of usage of cloud proxy solution?
- What is region-specific growth percentage of cloud proxy solution for Asia, Europe, and America?
- What is trend of moving MPLS to internet-based VPN solution?

7.4 METHODOLOGY

Since ISPs are providing high-speed internet with technological advancement of fiber to home to industrial broadband solution at affordable cost, more customers are adapting enterprise-level VPN service with additional tunnel to the cloud proxy for secure web browsing through homogeneous security policy across the organization with fewer exceptions.

The current study is based on secondary data of enterprise organizations that operate across the globe. Data span of last 5 years has been considered (2015–2019).

Major countries were analyzed for regions like South East Asia, Greater China, Pacific, Europe, Middle East, United Kingdom, Africa, North America, and South America, and findings will be documented and analyzed, and report will be generated to find greater visibility of the previous questions to present the trend of growth of the Internet in the recent years for site-to-site VPN connectivity in parallel to the MPLS connection and local internet breakout for faster access of cloud-hosted applications.

7.5 OBTAINED RESULTS

Based on sampling done upon the data collected from enterprise WAN connectivity, it has been seen in last 5-year span that there is a considerable amount of growth in the internet-based VPN connectivity, which has been increased around to 16% (Fig. 7.2).

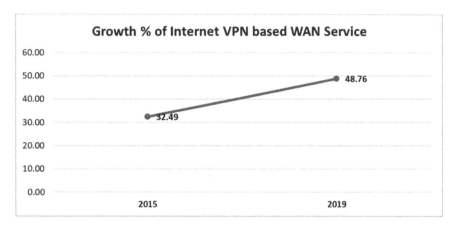

FIGURE 7.2   Growth of internet-based VPN services in last 5 years (2015–2019).

Increasing demand has been noticed on internet-based VPN connection that has replaced few MPLS-based WAN circuits, and the global MPLS has got decrement of around 15% (Figs. 7.3 and 7.4).

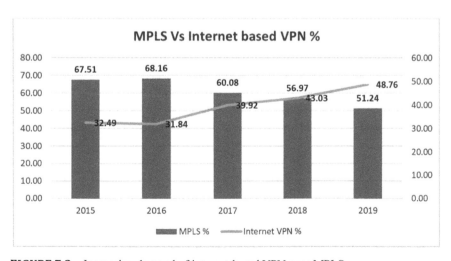

FIGURE 7.3   Increasing demand of internet-based VPN over MPLS.

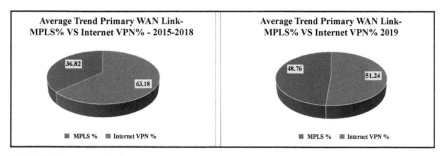

FIGURE 7.4   Trend of primary circuit—MPLS versus internet-based VPN percentage.

It has been interestingly noticed to reduce cost and getting advantage of local internet breakout through cloud proxy, and backup circuit of the sites has been moved from MPLS to internet-based VPN, as VPN router has got the capability to create two tunnels, for example—data tunnel for intranet connectivity and additional tunnel toward cloud proxy for secure web browsing or split tunnel and secure firewall communication for browsing and other internet-based application access (Fig. 7.5).

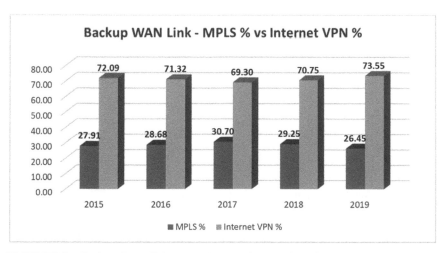

FIGURE 7.5   Backup WAN link—MPLS versus internet-based VPN percentage.

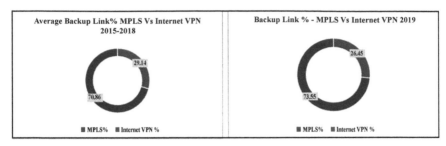

FIGURE 7.6   Increasing demand of backup link to be transformed to IPVPN.

There is a noticeable increase of around 4% in local internet breakout and secure web browsing through cloud proxy service across the globe in last 5-year span, which is aligned with the organizational transformation from legacy on-premises application access to next generation–ready cloud application (Fig. 7.6).

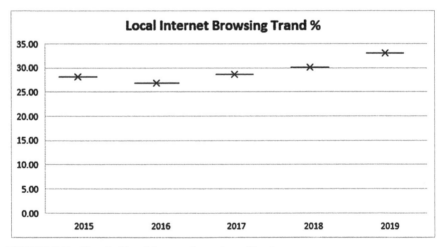

FIGURE 7.7   Trend of local internet browsing offload.

Across the globe, cloud proxy–based browsing and local internet offload have been initiated, Pacific and African regions have got relatively newer start, and advancement has been noticed in wider span in the American, European, and Asian regions (Figs. 7.7–7.9).

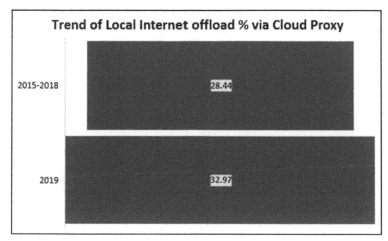

FIGURE 7.8   Trend of local internet browsing offload in last 5 years via cloud proxy.

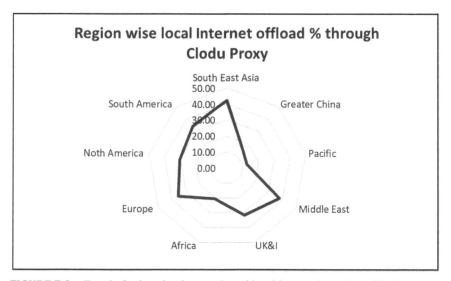

FIGURE 7.9   Trend of using cloud proxy–based local internet browsing offload.

7.6   CONCLUSIONS

To support easy and faster cloud-based application access, countries are moving toward internet-based VPN solution that provides flexibility of secure web browsing through cloud proxy. This transformation of WAN connectivity has got negative impact on the growth of international MPLS circuits.

The transformation from MPLS to internet-based VPN solution has got pros and cons. Cons mainly revolve around SLA of public internet connectivity, and since the Internet is purely uncontrolled no quality of service, application performance cannot be guaranteed and no end-to-end latency commitment is given from the ISPs.

Pros include low-cost solution with faster access to the cloud applications. The sites with MPLS connection with backup VPN connection or primary/backup VPN connection are ready to support future SD-WAN.

As the Internet has low SLA compared to MPLS connection, recommendation to the network administrator will be to go for enterprise-class internet connectivity with high availability assurance, preferably fiber optic–based connectivity compared to legacy DSL or leased line-based option. As long as the internet connection will be up, the VPN and web browsing service will be uninterrupted. High availability, greater uptime, and disaster readiness should be the key focus for the organization, so that they can achieve better reliability on the low-cost internet-based solution. Local ISP should make sure that the least cost path is delivered toward VPN gateway to enable faster routing over the Internet for intranet and internet access.

KEYWORDS

- cloud
- IoT
- WAN
- SD-WAN
- proxy
- MPLS
- IPVPN
- Internet
- SLA

REFERENCES

Sinha, S.; Das, A.; Ghosh, A. In *Importance of Technology and Cost Optimization for Wide Area Network (WAN) as Part of Sustainability Development*, International Conference Sustainability Development—A Value Chain Perspective, Management Development Institute (MDI), Sept 7–8, 2018.

Sinha, S.; Das, A.; Ghosh, A. In *WAN Technology and Cost Optimization Trend for UK and Ireland*, International Conference on Computational Techniques, Electronics and Mechanical Systems-CT EMS'18, Dec 21–23, 2018.

Sinha, S.; Das, A.; Ghosh, A. Importance of Standardization in Wide Area Network Capacity Management for Cost Optimization. *Int. J. Eng. Technol. (SCOPUS)* **2018,** *7* (2), 921–926. ISSN: 2227-524X.

Sinha, S.; Das, A.; Ghosh, A. Importance of Cost Analysis for International MPLS WAN. *Int. J. Recent Sci. Res.* **2018,** *9*, (7(G)), 28158–28161.

https://www.internetworldstats.com/emarketing.htm.

https://thenextweb.com/insider/2017/03/06/the-incredible-growth-of-the-internet-over-the-past-five-years-explained-in-detail/.

https://www.mckinsey.com/industries/high-tech/our-insights/the-great-transformer.

https://www.forbes.com/sites/bernardmarr/2018/05/21/how-much-data-do-we-create-every-day-the-mind-blowing-stats-everyone-should-read/#5a1ded5460ba.

https://www.statista.com/statistics/273018/number-of-internet-users-worldwide/.

https://thebestvpn.com/vpn-usage-statistics/.

https://www.vpnmentor.com/blog/vpn-use-data-privacy-stats/.

https://www.vpnmentor.com/blog/vital-internet-trends/.

CHAPTER 8

Blended IoT-Enabled Learning Approach to Raise the Gross Enrollment Ratio (GER) of Female Pupils: A Study Using a Clustering Technique

ANUPAM DAS[1], SAGAR KUMAR DHAWA[2], KRISHNADAS BANERJEE[3], AND ANIRBAN DAS[4*]

[1]*Department of Computer Science & Engineering, Amity University, Kolkata, India*

[2]*ICT/CS, J.C. Bose Institute of Education and Research, Bardhaman, West Bengal, India*

[3]*Jemes Academy, Kolkata, West Bengal, India*

[4]*Department of Computer Science, University of Engineering & Management, Kolkata, India*

*Corresponding author. E-mail: anirban-das@live.com

ABSTRACT

The GER of West Bengal in terms of female pupils' enrollments is very poor. As opined by the concerned female respondents, several reasons were identified as obstacles for them to carry on higher studies, leading to extremely fewer enrollments for higher studies in West Bengal. In this chapter, the most important causes of fewer gross enrollment ratios of female pupils are recognized through clustering technique, and the impacts of IoT-enabled learning to resolve the identified reasons are revealed.

8.1   INTRODUCTION

The United Nations demonstrates GER as a statistical measure to determine the education index of a region or nation. It is applicable to determine the enrollment of learners or pupils at elementary, middle, and high school levels.[2,7,10] In our society, it is observed that if a mother of a family is learned, definitely their girls become learned. It is because the learned mothers always try to make their girls educated. In any civilization, the education of female pupils is equally important as compared to male; failing which, the dropout rates of female pupils can never be controlled. West Bengal, a state of India, is our targeted state, and in this study, we will try to investigate the reasons for the low GER of female pupils. In addition, if we look at the year-wise attendance of pupils in higher education, we can see significant disparities among female and male pupils (Fig. 8.1).[4]

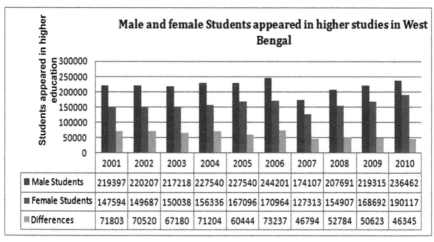

FIGURE 8.1 Number of pupils faced secondary examination in West Bengal (Ref: Report of Higher Education, Govt. of WB, 2010).

The district-wise enrollment record in higher education states poor GER of female pupils.

In Figure 8.2, A stands for Medinipur (E), B stands for 24 Parganas (S), C stands for Howrah, D stands for Hooghly, E stands for Burdwan, F stands for Purulia, G stands for Bankura, H stands for Medinipur (W),

I stands for Kolkata, J stands for 24 Parganas (N), K stands for Nadia, L stands for Murshidabad, M stands for Birbhum, N stands for Malda, O stands for Dinajpur (S), P stands for Dinajpur (N), Q stands for Jalpaiguri, R stands for Coochbehar, and S stands for Darjeeling.

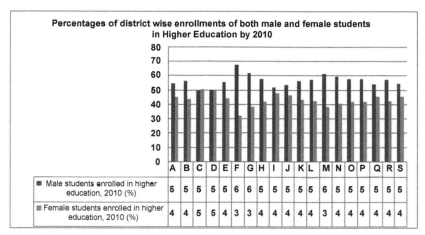

FIGURE 8.2   Enrollments in higher studies in WB in the year 2010.

8.2   LITERATURE REVIEW

Bista discussed several economic, psychological, institutional, social, and cultural barriers in higher studies for female pupils.[6] The GER of postsecondary pupils is 11% today in India, while the GER of rising nations is approximately more than 25%. Our nation had a plan to raise it to 15% almost by 2012 and 21% at the end of 12th Five years plan.[20] As per the statements of Mr. Sibal, we are targeting in escalating the GER to 30% by 2020. To accomplish this objective, it is required to skill 150 million young Indians.[19] Hati opines several indicators based on education in different stages of teaching and learning structure. He has made a compound Educational Development Index y.[32]

8.3   METHODOLOGY AND OUTCOME

Initially, a pilot approach to survey was held in Burdwan and Purba Medinipur, two districts of West Bengal. In t10 rural government-aided schools, female pupils of the secondary level were undergone randomly. They were asked to inform the obstacles they face in pursuing higher education. In the second phase, they were explained the details of learning through IoT-enabled learning methodologies, as a remedy to those obstacles in conventional higher education structure. Quite a few important points are revealed from pilot approach. On the basis of that final survey, the questionnaire was designed and applied to over 200 female pupils in different districts of West Bengal, that is, Paschim and Purba Medinipur, Howrah, Burdwan, Bankura, Purulia, South 24 Parganas, and Hooghly.

8.3.1   BARRIERS IN CONVENTIONAL HIGHER EDUCATION STRUCTURE[4]

The identified causes of fewer enrollments are reflected in Figure 8.3.

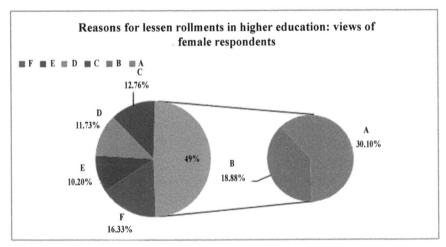

FIGURE 8.3   The identified causes of fewer enrollments as opined by female pupils.

Figure 8.3 represents that A is the poverty, B is the marriage before 18 years, C is the costly higher education, D is the lack of pressure from family, E is the no idea or directionless on higher education, and F is the other reasons (including inappropriate guidance, issues on public transportation, and distance from residence to college/school)

From Figure 8.3, it can be stated that the key factors responsible for less enrollments in higher studies are as follows:

1. Poverty
2. Family pressure for early marriage, expensive higher education
3. Improper guidance or motivation as they do not know why they should go for higher education
4. Lack of pressure from family

These four reasons cover almost 85% barriers. After listening to the reasons, the female pupils are asked whether they really support early marriage or not and whether early marriage is really a barrier to them in enrolling higher education. In response, 96% of female pupils supported that early marriage is an obstacle to enroll in higher education (Fig. 8.4).

Whether early marriage is really a barrier to female students in enrolling higher education

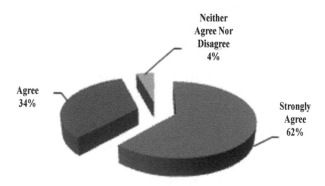

FIGURE 8.4 Responses of whether early marriage is really a barrier to female pupils in enrolling higher education: only female respondents.

Each female student was asked about the way outs so that these barriers, pointed by them, can be remedied. Several feedbacks regarding the solution came out, which are represented pictorially in Figure 8.5.

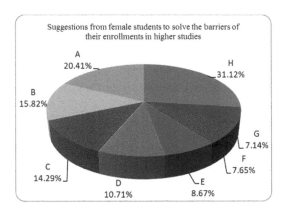

FIGURE 8.5   Suggestions from female pupils to solve the barriers to enrollments in higher studies.

In Figure 8.5, A is the awareness and counseling to both pupils and their parents, B is the scholarship and stipends for higher education, C is the free studentship for higher education, D is the awareness and counseling to pupils to get them interested in higher education, E is the government rules to reduce expenses of higher education, F is the early marriage control by following Govt. rules strictly, G is the essential economical development of this district, and H is the others (including development of public transportation system, establishment more higher education institutes nearer to locality, creation of job opportunities of family members within the district and allocate fund for drought-affected zone, make family members understood about girls' education).

From the views of the pupils regarding the solutions in terms of female pupils' enrollments in higher education, it can be concluded that general awareness is to be constructed in support of female pupils' higher education, controlling of early marriage, counseling of parents as well as female pupils about necessities of higher studies, progressive economic development of citizens, stipends, and scholarships.

8.3.2   IDENTIFICATION OF THE CAUSES OF LOW ENROLLMENTS THROUGH HIERARCHICAL CLUSTERING TECHNIQUE5

From the final survey, the obstacles to go for higher education by female pupils came out. The reasons are defined from R1 to R8:

R1: Poverty

R2: Engaged with family occupation

R3: Distance and transportation system connecting to residence and schools or colleges are not good

R4: Very few desired seats and less chance in higher education institutes for ordinary pupils

R5: Less interests in higher studies

R6: Improper guidance from family or school

R7: Politics in schools or colleges

R8: Job opportunities in retail-based industries

To pull the exact reasons, clustering approach (hierarchical) is enforced to authenticate the causes are prioritized.

Proximity matrix is shown in Table 8.1.

TABLE 8.1 Proximity Matrix.

Case	R1	R2	R3	R4	R5	R6	R7	R8
R1	0	633	448	191	583	124	145	772
R2	633	0	335	488	354	585	490	345
R3	448	335	0	385	321	392	439	422
R4	191	488	385	0	496	171	182	667
R5	583	354	321	496	0	527	518	315
R6	124	585	392	171	527	0	221	746
R7	145	490	439	182	518	221	0	643
R8	772	345	422	667	315	746	643	0

Table 8.2 reflects the agglomeration schedule.

TABLE 8.2 Average Linkage (Between Groups).

Stage	Cluster combined		Coefficients	Stage cluster first appears		Subsequent stage
	Cluster 1	Cluster 2		Cluster 1	Cluster 2	
1	1	6	125	0	0	2
2	1	4	180	1	0	3
3	1	7	181.66	2	0	7
4	5	8	314	0	0	6
5	2	3	334	0	0	6
6	2	5	359.5	5	4	7
7	1	2	549.75	3	6	0

Figure 8.6 shows dendrogram on the reasons as stated by the respondents.

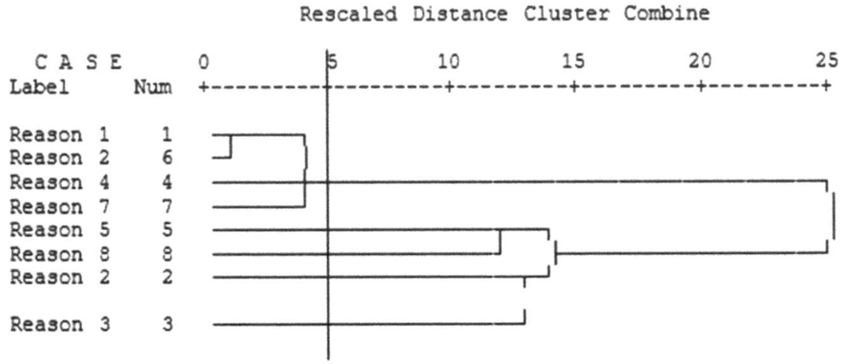

```
                        Rescaled Distance Cluster Combine

    C A S E      0        5        10        15        20        25
    Label     Num  +---------+---------+---------+---------+---------+

    Reason 1    1   ┐
    Reason 2    6   ┘
    Reason 4    4
    Reason 7    7
    Reason 5    5
    Reason 8    8
    Reason 2    2

    Reason 3    3
```

FIGURE 8.6   Dendrogram.

In Figure 8.6, the cluster analysis (hierarchical) equipped to five as distance via linkage (average) is measured. The causes such as R1, R6, R4, and R7 are framed in a cluster. The female respondents indicated mostly the reasons like R1, R6, R4, and R7 as the barriers to pursuing higher studies.

R1 indicates the reasons like poverty. R6 signifies improper guidance from family or school. R4 states that few desired seats and limited chance in colleges for ordinary pupils. R7 shows that involvements of politics affect the learning environment in institutes.

8.3.3   ESTABLISHMENT OF IOT-ENABLED LEARNING: FEMALE PUPILS' VIEW

While discussed about the concepts of IoT-enabled learning, all the female participants informed their eagerness to pursue higher studies via IoT applications as the majority of the problems get resolved through it. Though IoT learning applications can resolve some issues, still they were asked whether any problems may occur in enrolling or pursuing higher studies. In response, some issues reflected are represented in Figure 8.7.

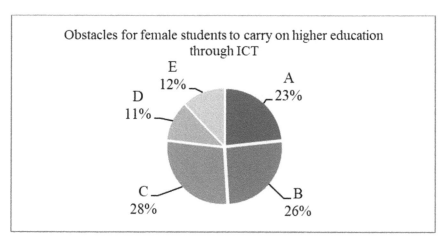

FIGURE 8.7   Obstacles for female pupils to carry on higher education through IoT-enabled learning.

In Figure 8.7, the ordinates represent that A is the family members who think more for the education of boys with respect to girls, B is the family members who are unaware of IoT-enabled learning that may lead to their unwillingness to send their girl pupils to go for it, C is the early marriage, as before getting into higher education, they are forced for marriage, D is that they do not know why they should go for it, and E is the female pupils who are deprived of education as they are too busy with homework.

To interpret the obstacles for female pupils to carry on higher studies through IoT, it is transparent that awareness regarding IoT-enabled higher education is to be spread to parents as well as female pupils so that parents do not do gender discrimination in the case of higher education and do not force female pupils in early marriage and pupils get a ray of hope to build their career through IoT-based higher education.

The female pupils were asked regarding their suggestions to overcome the obstacles and to carry on higher education through IoT. They suggested some solutions that are diagrammatically represented in Figure 8.8.

The ordinates in Figure 8.8 depict that A is the counseling and aware-ness to family members for the necessity of girls' higher education through IoT, B is the proposal to make family members convinced that girl pupils also have the competence to grow simultaneously like boys and they can also flourish if opportunities are given, C is the proper utilization of government rules to control early marriage, D is the proper guidance of higher education is required, and E is the IoT classes that should be fixed according to the female student's time.

Suggestions to overcome the obstacles for female students to carry on higher education through e-learning

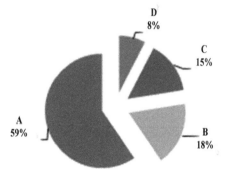

FIGURE 8.8   Suggestions by female-student respondents to overcome the obstacles and to carry on higher education through IoT-based learning.

It is stressed, based on IoT, that the awareness about female education and counseling of parents/family members are held so that the guardians as well as their wards can feel the importance of higher studies and the female pupils are not forced for marriage at an early age.

8.4   CONCLUSION

The obstacles experienced by the female pupils in pursuing higher education in West Bengal were extracted. From these, few causes/reasons were obtained via hierarchical clustering methodology. The intention is to remove those major obstacles so that the GER of the female pupils will increase exceedingly. IoT-enabled learning practices are employed here as the best possible way outs from the said key factors of fewer enrollments in higher studies. Pupils wholeheartedly accepted IoT-based studies after getting well acquainted. Finally, the application of ICT can improve the GER of female pupils in West Bengal.

KEYWORDS

- **higher education**
- **gross enrollment ratio**
- **IoT-enabled learning**
- **hierarchical clustering technique**

REFERENCES

1. Annual Report. Ministry of Higher Education, Govt. of West Bengal, 2011.
2. Banerjee, N.; Mukherjee, M. *The Changing Status of Women in West Bengal, 1970–2000: The Challenge Ahead.*
3. Basu, A.; Mandal, A.; Das, A. Blueprint of the Graphical Galaxy of Solar System Segment: An Algorithmic Approach Using CSS3.0. *Global J. Adv. Res.* **2015,** *1* (1).
4. Bijlani, K.; Guntha, R.; Pai, C. S.; George, S.; Subramanian, S. In *Talk to a Teacher-Ecosystem for Synchronous Online Interaction with a Large set of Pupils,* 2nd International Conference on e-Education, e-Business, e-Management and ICT (IC4E 2011), 2011.
5. Bista, M. B. *A Review of Research Literature on Girls' Education in Nepal.* Aug 2004.
6. Chouni, S.; Paul, N.; Das, A.; A Graphical-pseudo-algorithmic Approach to Evaluate Shortest Route Maps of Indian Railway Stations. *Int. J. Innov. Technol. Adapt. Manage.* **2014,** *1* (7).
7. Das, A.; et al. A Cutting-Edge Approach in Bridging between Microsoft.NET Framework and SAP R/3. *Int. J. Comput. App.* **2011,** (4), Article 3 [ISSN: 0975-8887].
8. Das, A. Identification of Reasons of Low GER of Higher Education of Rural Female Pupils Using Clustering Technique: ICT Based Education as a Plausible Way Out. *Int. J. Adv. Sci. Technol.* **2016,** *96.*
9. Das, A. Impact of ICT to Enhance the GER of Higher Education of Female Pupils in West Bengal. *Persp. Manage. Heritage Bus. School* **2013,** *5* (1 & 2).
10. Das, A.; Banerjee D.K.; Basu K. Implementation of ICT in West Bengal to Enhance the Present GER in Higher Education. *Int. J. Innov. Manage. Technol.* **2011,** *2* (3).
11. Das, A.; Banerjee, D. K.; Basu, K. Implementation of ICT in West Bengal to Enhance the Present GER in Higher Education. *Int. J. Innov. Manage. Technol. [IJIMT]* **2011,** *2* (3), 257–261
12. Das, A.; Banerjee, D. K.; Basu, K. Model ICT Web Portal Targeting to Enhance GER of Higher Education in West Bengal. *Int. J. Inf. Edu. Technol. (IJIET)* **2012,** *2* (1), 43–47.
13. Das, A.; Das, A.; Banerjee D. K.; et al. In *Best Practices for Enhancing Downloading Speed of Ecommerce/ICT Websites,* International Symposium on Devices MEMS, Intelligent Systems & Communication (ISDMISC); Sikkim, India, 2011.

14. Das, A.; Dhawa, S. K.; Banerjee, K.; Das, A. An Empirical Study and Recommendations to Improve GER of West Bengal. *Int. J. Eng. Sci. Technol. Res. (SCOPUS)* **2018**, *3* (3), 17–26; ISSN: 2456-0464.

15. Das, A.; Gupta, S. An Empirical Analysis to Determine Poverty as Key Issue of Fewer Enrollments: ICT as the Best Remedy to Enhance GER of Higher Studies in West Bengal. *Int. J. Comput. Theory Eng. (IJCTE)* **2011**, *3* (6).

16. Das, A.; Halder, C.; et al. In *LP Based Model to Find Optimal Portfolio to Maximize the Profit in Software Project Billing*, Second International Conference on Green Computing and Internet of Things (ICGCIoT 2018) sponsored by IEEE; Thomson Reuters & SCOPUS, August 16–19, 2018.

17. Das, A.; Nandi, S.; Basu, K. Enhancement of Gross Enrollment Ratio of Higher Education of West Bengal through ICT: A Fuzzy Delphi Forecasting Approach. *Int. J. Soc. Sci. Humanity (IJSSH)* **2011**, *1* (4), 278–284.

18. Das, A.; Nandi, S.; Basu, K. Enhancement of Gross Enrolment Ratio of Higher Education of West Bengal through ICT: A Fuzzy Delphi Forecasting Approach. *Int. J. Soc. Sci. Humanity (IJSSH)* **2011**, *1* (4), 278–284.

19. Das, A.; Panigrahi, G.; Basu, K. An Approach to Propose a Model for ICT Content Up-Gradation for Increasing GER of Higher Education in West Bengal. *Procedia— Soc. Behav. Sci.* **2011**, *28*, 333–336.

20. Das, A.; Patra, S.; Basu, K.; Banerjee, D. K. A Study to Determine the Higher Education Enrolments of West Bengal Prior to and Subsequent to Incorporation of ICT: A Discriminant Analysis Approach. *Int. J. e-Edu., e-Busi., e-Manage. ICT (IJEEEE)* **2011**, *1* (4).

21. Das, A.; Patra, S.; Basu, K.; Banerjee, D. K. In *Identification of the Reasons of Low GER of Higher Education in West Bengal: A Hierarchical Clustering Technique*, Presented in International Conference on Operations Research for Sustainable Development in Globalized Environment by ORSI; India, 2012.

22. Das, A.; Patra, S.; Basu, K.; Banerjee, D. K. In *Identification of the Reasons of Low GER of Higher Education in West Bengal: A Hierarchical Clustering Technique*, Presented in International Conference on Operations Research for Sustainable Development in Globalized Environment; ORSI Proceedings 2012 by Operations Research Society of India, India, 2012.

23. Das, A.; Patra, S.; Basu, K.; Banerjee, D. K. A Study to Determine the Higher Education Enrollments of West Bengal Prior to and Subsequent to Incorporation of ICT: A Discriminant Analysis Approach. *Int. J. e-Edu., e-Busi., e-Manage. ICT (IJEEEE)* **2011**, *1* (4).

24. Das, A.; Sau, A.; Panigrahi, G. Web Attributes Offered by Websites of Universities of West Bengal to Run ICT System: A Hierarchical Clustering Based Study. *J. Comput. Sci. Syst. Biol. 8* (4).

25. Das, A.; Gupta, S.; Bandopadhyay, P.; Nandan, M. In *A Study To Determine Poverty as a Key Factor for Less Enrollments in Higher Education through eLearning in West Bengal and Allocation of Funds by Means of e-Monitoring as a Best Solution Using Web Enabled Applications*. International Conference on Emerging Trends in Networks and Communications [ETNCC 2011]; Udaipur, India, 2015.

26. GOI. Report of the National Commission for Religious and Linguistic Minorities; Ministry of Minority Affairs, Government of India, May 2007.

27. GOI. Social, Economic and Educational Status of the Muslim Community of India – A Report; Prime Minister's High-Level Committee, Cabinet Secretariat, Government of India, November 2006.

28. Hati, K. K. *Socio-Religious Disparity in Educational Achievements: A District Level Study in West Bengal, National Seminar on Emerging Issues in Indian Economy.* Rabindra Bharati University, 2010.

29. Honey, P. ICT: A Performance Appraisal and Some Suggestions for Improvement. *Learn. Org.* **2001,** *8* (5), 200–202; prepared for UNESCO, Bangkok.

30. Kanbargi, R. *Equity in Education in Karnataka.* Education Department, Government of Karnataka: Bangalore, 2000.

31. Colossal Wastage of Human Resources in West Bengal. *Mainstream* **2008,** *XLVI* (14)

32. Panigrahi, G.; Das, A. Technological and Design Up-Gradation of Indian Tourist Websites for Better Marketability, SURVEY. *Indian Instit. Soc. Welf. Busi. Manage. (IISWBM), Kolkata* **2009,** *49* (1 & 2).

33. Panigrahi, G.; Das, A.; Basu, K. In *A Problem Centric Clustering of Educational Website Attributes to Increase GER of Higher Education in West Bengal,* Presented in International Conference on Operations Research for Sustainable Development in Globalized Environment; ORSI Proceedings 2012 by Operations Research Society of India, India, 2012.

34. Panigrahi, G.; Das, A.; Basu, K. A Study to Increase Effectiveness of Distance Learning Websites in India with Special Reference to the State West Bengal to Increase the Present GER of Higher Education through Incorporation of ICT Facility in a Better Way. *Procedia—Soc. Behav. Sci.* **2011,** *15,* 1535–1539.

35. Panigrahi, G.; Das, A.; Basu, K. A Study to Make a Clustering of Website Attributes on User Interface to Increase the Effectiveness of Indian Educational Websites. *Int. J. Edu. Res. Technol.* Sept **2012,** *3* (3), 32–36.

36. Panigrahi, G.; Das, A.; Basu, K. In *A Study Towards Building an Optimal Graph Theory Based Model for the Design of Tourism Website,* International Conference on Modeling, Optimization & Computing [ICMOC 2010]; National Institute of Technology, Durgapur, India-Proceedings published in American Institute of Physics [AIP], 2010.

37. Panigrahi, G.; Das, A.; Basu, K. A Survey on ICT Attributes of University Websites of Different Countries. *Int. J. Edu. Res. Technol.* **2012,** *3* (3), 13–15.

38. Wikipedia–Definition of Gross Enrollment Ratio; Dated Nov 1, 2011.

CHAPTER 9

IoT-Enabled Garbage Disposal System with Advanced Message Notification System through Android Application

PAROMITA MITRA[1*], AMARJEET SINGH[2], and RAJDEEP CHOWDHURY[3]

[1]KGS Technology Group, Kolkata, West Bengal, India

[2]Global Institute of Technology, Gurgaon, Haryana, India

[3]Chinsurah, Hooghly 712101, West Bengal, India

*Corresponding author. E-mail: mitrapm121097@gmail.com

ABSTRACT

Our earth is presently dealing with a large number of problems. Each and every invention of humans has its repercussion that the earth has to face, and we too as being a part of the earth have to face it. The generation of solid waste is one such issue and so is its disposal. Our work is an aid to make this disposal more organized, hygienic, and coordinated together with the help of government cleaning staff. The Witty Bin can be considered as a dustbin that has wits or intelligence. It is a compact device that is sensor enabled. This bin is able to notify the government staff about the dustbin getting filled up and send a location-based emergency message to clean it up. The metal detector sensor enables the bin to notify about the possible bomb droppings. The dustbin also conveys an assumption-based message about the possible contents of the dustbin. This assumption is based on the mathematical calculation involving some sensors. The work is a unique solution for a cleaner society. The municipality staff could act more efficiently, making their work more significant and recognizable in society.

9.1   INTRODUCTION

The solid waste management has received great attention in recent times. The reason behind this is quite simple. The huge human population with its huge needs is creating new things each day. And as we know, everything has its left over of it its own way, be it living or nonliving. The generation of this huge waste requires a good and proper process of disposing them off and also a great management to remove them from each corner of the society. The government nowadays is very keen for cleaning society and is launching movements for it. There are many such movements. A particular one that has been directed by our honorable prime minister is the "Swachh Bharat" movement. This movement was successful in many ways and has inspired many people inculcating the good habit of disposing waste in dustbins. But with more people getting aware of dumping garbage in dustbins and making the surrounding cleaner, the dustbins are getting used up more. First, a problem occurred in the starting of this problem is the shortage of dustbins everywhere. But now with the government intervention, there are an adequate number of dustbins, but still the problem persists. With huge number of people dumping their waste in dustbins, these bins are getting filled up very fast and thus require a removal of these wastes by the government staff. But even after such a successful movement, no steps have been taken to improve or to make the municipality staff working more efficient. The work is a way to support this wonderful movement of our government and helping to cope with this lag behind of this movement. The Witty Bin is sensor-enabled smart device together with an Android application. The smart dustbin is able to provide important information to the cleaning staff, making their work much easy and efficient. The work will have the following parts and will concentrate on the following issues:

- The efficient notification—The Witty Bin will send important information about the dustbin getting filled up. This will make the work of the cleaning staff much efficient and will also not allow the garbage to spill on the ground or on the road. This issue is quite common, and with these kinds of things taking place, the motive of dustbins is not fulfilled even after people getting aware of their dumping habits.
- The smart sensors—The dustbins are sometime served as a way to dump many inappropriate things such as a bomb. It has been seen

that many blasts have taken place in our country where bombs were hidden inside the dustbin; the sensor-enabled Witty Bin is able to notify about a possible bomb dropping. Also, there are sensors that, with the help of a calculative approach, will give an assumption-based information about contents of the bin. Also, there are level indicator sensors that show that the dustbin is getting filled up.

- The Android application—The smart dustbin is designed together with an Android application. The application will allow a location-based notification of the bins getting filled up along with the given information.

9.2 OBJECTIVE

This work aims at the design of a user-friendly cognitive dustbin. The Witty Bin can be a revolution in the field of intelligent devices. The product could build up a healthy and clean society. The objective is to integrate electronics and smart device concept into the common household products to make them more suitable as per modern needs. The "Witty Bin" can be a blessing for smart cities. The concept is mainly to stop the overfilling of the dustbins and thus prevent the garbage from spilling on the road or the site where the dustbin is located.

9.3 PROPOSED WORK

9.3.1 PURPOSE OF DUSTBIN

A **waste container** is basically a container for temporarily storing waste and is usually made out of metal or plastic. Some common terms are **dustbin**, **garbage can**, and **trash can**. The words "rubbish," "basket," and "bin" are more common in British English usage; "trash" and "can" are more common in American English usage. "Garbage" may refer to domestic waste specifically (when distinguished from "trash") or to municipal solid waste in general. In 1875, the first household rubbish bins or dustbins were introduced in Britain to create a regulated system of collection.

The dustbin thus has an important position in our daily life. We aimed at making this device smart, as smart as our new human society.

The dustbin is a very old entity. Our intelligent solution provides a whole lot of new and smart features.

Our first concern was the spilling of garbage due to overfilling, especially during festive seasons. We often find that the dustbins are overfilled and thus spreading garbage all over. In this case, the purpose of dustbin is not getting fulfilled.

Thus, our dustbin provides a solution by indicating the level of garbage. The level is indicated in form of percentage, so the dustbin knows exactly when to stop accepting the garbage inputs.

The buzzer will allow people to understand that the bin is full. Also, it would stop them from continuing throwing garbage into the same bin.

The pressure sensors enable to guess us the weight. Based on the weight, there would be a calculative indication of the probable contents of the dustbins.

The Witty Bin simply uses the relation between pressure, volume, and weight. The volume of the bin will be known to us, the pressure will be calculated by the pressure sensors below, and the weight will be hence calculated. The relational formulae to be used are

$$P = F/A$$

$$D = M/V$$

where P = pressure, F = force, A = area = volume = mass

The output data on the display or the mobile notification will be based on the calculative data. The assumption-based data will be controlled by microprocessor (Table 9.1).

TABLE 9.1 Assumption for Weight–Pressure Calculation.

Contents	Weight
Glass	Up to 3 kg
Plastic	Up to 2 kg
Vegetables	Up to 5 kg
Metal	Up to 8 kg
Random	Up to 10 kg

The metal detector sensor will indicate the presence of metal waste inside the dustbin. This indication helps us to stay alert against possible bomb droppings and helps us to curb attacking attempts by terrorist.

All the functions are coded in Arduino UNO, which enables us to get an automated function.

The Android application module will work specially for the cleaning staff. The Android application will be the point of contact between the Witty Bin and the municipality people. It will convey all the important notifications along with the location-based message of the overflowing dustbin. Other information includes the indication of possible bomb dropping and the assumption-based notification about the contents of the dustbin.

The sensor-enabled lid—As we have used multiple ultrasonic sensors, we have used one specifically for the automatic sensor-enabled lid of the dustbin. The bin senses the presence of someone in front and immediately opens up for disposal of garbage. The lid again takes its usual position after some time (Figs. 9.1 and 9.2).

FIGURE 9.1   The level indication of garbage in form of percentage.

FIGURE 9.2   Witty Bin with its sensor-enabled lid (open and close positions).

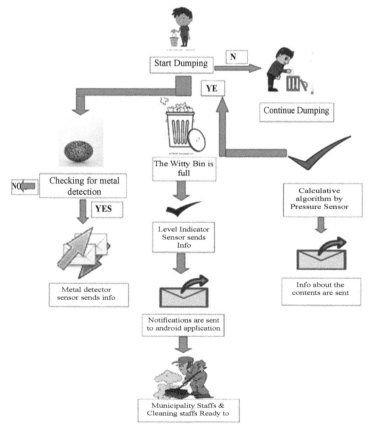

FIGURE 9.3   Picture representation of the workflow diagram.

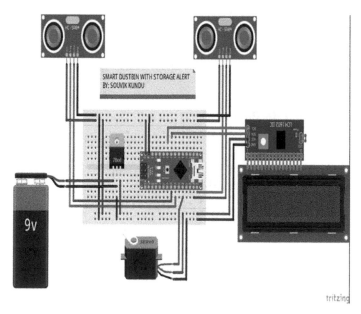

FIGURE 9.4   Main circuit diagram for this work.

The workflow diagram shows the picture representation of the proposed way of working of the device or bin. The process starts as we start dumping garbage into the bin. The bin shows an indication in percentage. With the help of this indication, we can understand the scope of the bin and that how much more garbage it can hold or store (Fig. 9.3).

During the dumping process if any metal is dropped, the metal detector sensor present in the bin will immediately detect it and send a notification to the municipality staff. Not all metal droppings will be hazardous or dangerous. But definitely it will help the staff to stay alert about the thing. Also, this system will help us to stay alert during high-alert situations when the country faces threats and becomes vulnerable to terrorist attacks (Fig. 9.4).

The pressure sensor module will help us to calculate the weight of the dumped garbage. Based on the weight, there would be a simple assumption-based algorithm to suggest the kind of material dumped into the bin. The data will be highly on assumption and can be more accurately guessed with the help of material sensor and segregation system.

After the bin gets full, it gives a buzzer and with the help of an Internet of Things (IoT)-enabled system sends a location-based notification that the bin is full and would require immediate cleaning. After the cleaning action is done, the bin condition is again turned to normal.

9.3.2 CODE FOR THE PROJECT

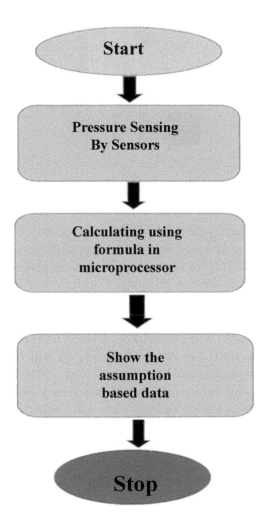

```
#include <Wire.h>
#include<Servo.h>
#include<LiquidCrystal_I2C.h>

Servo servo;
LiquidCrystal_I2C lcd(0x27, 16, 2);
 // defines pins numbers
 const int pos = 20;

 const int echoPin = 11; //Checking storage
 const int trigPin = 12; //Checking storage

 const int echoPin1 = 5; //Checking cap status
 const int trigPin1 = 6; //Checking cap status

 const int servoPin = 8;

 // defines variables
 long duration, duration1;
 int distance, distance1;

void setup() {
 Serial.begin(9600); // Starts the serial communication
 lcd.begin(); // Starts the lcd communication
 servo.attach(servoPin);
 pinMode(trigPin, OUTPUT); // Sets the trigPin as an Output
 pinMode(echoPin, INPUT); // Sets the echoPin as an Input
 pinMode(trigPin1, OUTPUT); // Sets the trigPin1 as an Output
 pinMode(echoPin1, INPUT); // Sets the echoPin1 as an Input
 servo.write(pos);
 delay(100);
 servo.detach();
 lcd.setCursor(1,0);
 lcd.print("SMART DUSTBIN");
 lcd.setCursor(1,1);
 lcd.print("USING ARDUINO");
 delay(2000);
 lcd.clear();
```

```
  }

void loop() {
  checkvol();
  lcd.clear();

  // for checking storage
  digitalWrite(trigPin, LOW);
  delayMicroseconds(2);
  digitalWrite(trigPin, HIGH);
  delayMicroseconds(10);
  digitalWrite(trigPin, LOW);
  duration = pulseIn(echoPin, HIGH);
  distance = duration*0.034/2;

  //for opening/closing the dustbin cap
  digitalWrite(trigPin1, LOW);
  delayMicroseconds(2);
  digitalWrite(trigPin1, HIGH);
  delayMicroseconds(10);
  digitalWrite(trigPin1, LOW);
  duration1 = pulseIn(echoPin1, HIGH);
  distance1 = duration1*0.034/2;

  if ( distance1<40 ) {
    servo.attach(servoPin);
    delay(1);
    servo.write(pos+160);
    lcd.setCursor(3,0);
    lcd.print("CAP OPENED");
    delay(1000);
    lcd.clear();
    servo.write(pos);
    lcd.setCursor(3,0);
    lcd.print("CAP CLOSED");
    delay(1000);
    lcd.clear();
  }
```

```
    else {
       servo.write(0);
     }
     delay(300);
  }
  //End of main loop


  // Function for checking container storage
  void checkvol() {
    if (distance>=25){
       lcd.print("DUSTBIN IS EMPTY");
       delay(2000);
    }

    else if (distance>=15){
       lcd.setCursor(4,0);
       lcd.print("25% FULL");
       delay(2000);
    }

    else if (distance>=10){
      lcd.setCursor(4,0);
       lcd.print("50% FULL");
       delay(2000);
    }

    else if (distance=10){
       lcd.setCursor(4,0);
       lcd.print("75% FULL");
       delay(2000);
    }

    else if (distance>=5){
       lcd.setCursor(4,0);
       lcd.print("100% FULL");
       delay(2000);
    }
```

```
    else{
      lcd.setCursor(2,0);
      lcd.print("_____");
      delay(2000);
      lcd.clear();
  }
}
```

9.4   CONCLUSION

Thus, the Witty Bin is not only an entirely new approach to the society but also can be called the need of the hour. When the whole country is moving toward a clean and better tomorrow, it can be the best way to share our contribution. As already mentioned, it makes the cleaning staff's work more efficient and thus more recognizable. Mostly it happens that the cleaning staff's contribution is neglected, but this technology will allow them to come forward and show their efficiency. This introduced technology will also increase the security to some extent as the metal detector sensor could hint the presence of bomb. This could alert the staff and the security persons and can curb blasts. Witty Bin can also be very useful in inspiring people to use dustbins. Moreover, the dustbins will be very clean as they will be timely emptied, and the garbage will also not spill. This will result in low contamination level in society, leading toward a healthy and cleaner society.

The concept thus formed can have multiple dimensions of application in near future. Many more features can be added to it to make it smarter and apt for modern lifestyle.

9.5   FUTURE SCOPE

The product has a great scope in the future, with lots of new aids and dimensions added to it. The "Witty Bin" is already an intelligent dustbin and prevents garbage spilling, leading a step toward a healthy society. The bin is sensor enabled and includes common-sensor equipment. With more sophisticated sensors adding to it, it could become more cognitive in nature and can serve better. Such a kind of sensor is the material sensor. This sensor will not only make the bin understand the garbage type dropped in it but can be useful in segregation of the garbage based on the understanding. This can also lead a more positive use. In our society, we can often see cases where unwanted children are dropped in dustbins or small animals getting trapped in dustbins. The material sensor and advanced monitoring system will allow us to curb these problems.

The GPS-based message notification to the municipality staff through Android application will enable a timely cleaning of the bins with the intervention of IoT concept.

KEYWORDS

- **IoT**
- **Arduino UNO**
- **ultrasonic**
- **Android**
- **sensor**

REFERENCES

Abdoli, S. RFID Application in Municipal Solid Waste Management System, University of Tehran, Aug 14, 2009.

Borozdukhin, A.; Dolinina, O.; Pechenkin, V. Approach to the Garbage Collection in the Smart Clean City Project, *Yuri Gagarin State Technical University of Saratov, Saratov, Russia*, 2016.

Catania, V.; Ventura, D. In *An Approach for Monitoring and Smart Planning of Urban Solid Waste Management Using Smart-M3 Platform*, Proceedings of 15th Conference of Open Innovations Association FRUCT, 2014; pp 24–31.

Chowdhury, B.; Chowdhury, M. U. In *RFID-Based Real-Time Smart Waste Management System, 2007 Australasian Telecommunication Networks and Applications Conference*, Dec 2–5, 2007.

Dey, S.; Kundu, T. Web Based Real-Time Home Automation and Security System. *IJEETC* **2015,** *4* (3).

Flora, A. *Towards a Clean Environment: A Proposal on Sustainable and Integrated Solid Waste Management System for University Kebangsaan Malaysia; Report from Alam Flora*, 2009.

Gubbi, J.; Buyya, R.; Marusic, S.; Palaniswami, M. Internet of Things (IoT): A Vision, Architectural Elements, and Future Directions. **2013,** *29* (7), 1645–1660.

Hannan, A. M.; Arebey, M.; Basri, H. Intelligent Solid Waste Bin Monitoring and Management System. *Aust. J. Basic Appl. Sci. 2010*, *4* (10), 5314–5319.

Hong, I.; Park, S.; Lee, B.; Lee, J.; Jeong, D.; Park, S. IoT-Based Smart Garbage System for Efficient Food Waste Management, Aug 28, 2014.

Hong, I.; Park, S.; Lee, B.; Lee, J.; Jeong, D.; Park, S. IoT-Based Smart Garbage System for Efficient Food Waste Management. *Sci. World J.* **2014**, *2014*, 646953.

Longhi, S.; Marzioni, D.; Alidor, E.; Di Bu'o, G.; Prist, M.; Grisostomi, M.; Pirro, M. Solid Waste Management Architecture Using Wireless Sensor Network Technology, *Universit`aPolitecnicadelle Marche, Dipartimento di Ingegneriadell'. Informazione Via BrecceBianche. Snc, 60131 Ancona, Italy*, 2012.

Medvedev, A.; Fedchenkov, P.; Zaslavsky, A.; Anagnostopoulos, T.; Khoruzhnikov, S. Waste Management as an IoT-Enabled Service in Smart Cities. In *Lecture Notes in Computer Science (Including Subseries Lecture Notes in Artificial Intelligence and Lecture Notes in Bioinformatics)*; 2015; Vol. 9247, pp 104–115.

Navghane, S. S.; Killedar, M. S.; Rohokale, V. M. IoT Based Smart Garbage and Waste Collection Bin. *Int. J. Adv. Res. Electron. Commun. Eng.* **2016**, *5* (5), 1576–1578.

Perera, C.; Zaslavsky, A.; Christen, P.; Georgakopoulos, D. Sensing as a Service Model for Smart Cities Supported by Internet of Things. **2014**, *25* (1), 81–93.

Sharma, N.; Singha, N.; Dutta, T. Smart Bin Implementation for Smart Cities. *Int. J. Sci. Eng. Res.* **2015**, *6* (9), 787–791.

CHAPTER 10

IoT-Based Self-Healing Concrete (SHC): Using Bacteria and Environmental Waste

SUNIT KUMAR SINGH[1*], SATYAM KUMAR SINGH[1], and
RAJDEEP CHOWDHURY[2]

[1]*Department of Civil Engineering, JIS College of Engineering,
Kalyani 741235, Nadia, West Bengal, India*

[2]*Chinsurah 712101, Hooghly, West Bengal, India*

Corresponding author. E-mail: 13596sunit@gmail.com

ABSTRACT

Concrete is a vital material for resisting applied load on it, but if the applied load on concrete is higher than the resisting load, a serious problem occurs that damages the life of buildings by producing crack in concrete. Concrete is the mostly used material in construction. However, it has some disadvantages like carbon dioxide gas produced from cracks developed in concrete, which directly gives bad impact on our environment. Cracks in concrete are one of the implicit weaknesses through which water and other substances percolate, introducing corrosion, and thus slowly retards the life of concrete. Not to mention that large sums of fortune are being spent to maintain the concrete work. If crack formation in concrete is not taken care of, then life of buildings would be reduced, which may cause lots of problem in the future. Different sizes of crack develop in concrete that need to be repair manually; it will help in preventing shortening of the life of concrete. It is said that concrete is like the backbone of a building. Crack formation is very common in concrete, which decreases strength, durability, and workability. Here, durability term is directly related to strength of concrete, and it is defined as to maintaining its engineering properties in weathering conditions, chemical attacks, etc. It specifies the length of the life of concrete. Degree of durability depends upon different types of concrete depending on environment. For example, in coastal areas, the need of concrete will be subjected to distinct demands in comparison of concrete used in other areas. Not only it affects the concrete, but also it affects reinforcement also when it comes in contact with substances like hydrogen dioxide, carbon dioxide, and other reacting agents. Repair of crack developed in concrete demands maintenance and various types of treatment that is very expensive. Therefore, to avoid all these problems, self-healing approaches are introduced into the concrete work, which will be helpful for repairing of concrete biologically (using microorganisms and environment waste) and by chemically (using reacting agents). Self-healing techniques in cementitious materials will help to enhance the life of concrete. One of them is "microencapsulation" (it is the process in which tiny particles are merged with glue and are surrounded by the coating of small capsule containing many useful properties. Capsules can also be used to fit in solids, liquids, and gases. Coated material of capsule is made up of ethyl cellulose, polyvinyl alcohol, etc.), which is the best self-healing method, where these microcapsules break and release healing agent in cracks. Here, one thing should also notice that sodium silicate plays a great role as self-healing agent in cementitious material. Also, for enhancing the engineering cement structure, characteristics are substituted by concrete constructions bacteria like *Bacillus pseudofirmus*. Huge variety of bacteria are present in the nature, and according to their living conditions, some of bacteria can survive in alkaline environment such as *Bacillus sphaericus* and *Bacillus subtilis*. Different bacterial types have different condition of growth. Bacteria help to improve structural properties like strength, permeability, and durability of concrete. According to research, it was found that the aggregate of light weight together with bacteria enables to self-healing concrete properties. The work is all about healing process of concrete. Since it is a matter of research and analytics, we found that the types of concrete are different; thus, the healing processes are also different. We had used quality analysis and reporting for the materials where quality analysis is done by a tool, and depending on that, we can decide what kind of healing techniques should be used to overcome the problem. The following generated data will ultimately get accumulated to form a database that suggests a type of cement available in the market and the types of fault that can be dealt with. The work is meant for detection of cracks by crack detection sensor or fiber-optic sensing system. The information is conveyed with a location-based message to the municipality authorities. The sensor together with Internet of things forms a system that enables quick repair of roads with the application of self-healing cement.

10.1 INTRODUCTION

The word concrete is originated from the Latin word "concretus" that means condensed and hardened. The earliest use of cement is dated back to 12,000 years ago, although the early use of concrete-like building material is dated back to 6500 B.C. However, it was not formed as concrete until later during the Roman Empire. As it was pioneering, lime-based cement had a shorter lifespan due to its vulnerability to forming cracks. It is inventive to receive carbonate precipitation initiated by microbes to fill the splits. The technique, which is an aftereffect of organic exercises, is normal and free of contamination. The microbial precipitation depends on a number of factors, including dissolved inorganic carbon concentration, pH and calcium ion concentration, and nucleation sites. Also, when bacteria are used to heal cracks in concrete, the main obstacle factor is the high-alkaline concrete environment that restricts the bacteria's growth. Therefore, necessary measures are needed to be taken to protect bacteria in concrete. So, to ensure effective mineral precipitation that may lead to crack healing, care should be taken to fulfill the preconditions. It is a new and promising method, and the research in this aspect is currently more focused on the durability side, while the mechanical properties are somewhat touched and further research needs to be carried out. There are many researchers who are trying to improve the concrete to get a better longevity among many others. That is how the concept of self-healing finds its way to concrete (Fig. 10.1).

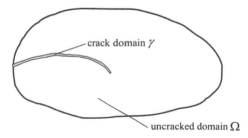

FIGURE 10.1   Crack domain (Y) and uncracked domain (Ω).

When it comes to developing this kind of concrete, there are two primary characteristic areas of research: the cracks over time and the artificial method to seal cracks, which needs workability and durability. This will have a huge positive impact on both the environment and economics. On the other hand, it might improve the architectural designs by forcing new design methods, and hence, it changes the shape of internal spaces, so that it serves many features and provides flexibility. The material concrete is considered to be very good for resisting compressive load to a limit, but if the load on the concrete exceeds its resistant load limit, the strength of the concrete is reduced by forming the cracks in the concrete and the crack treatment becomes very expensive. Not only does the repair become expensive, but also the properties such as durability, permeability, and concrete strength are reduced. The increase in concrete permeability leads to concrete bleeding and comes into contact with strengthening concrete structure, which causes corrosion and rusting after some time. Due to this, strength of concrete structure decreases rapidly, which shows the necessity to repair cracks.

10.1.1   DEFINITION OF SELF-HEALING CONCRETE (SHC)

A material that is self-healed can be considered as a material that can repair itself to the initial state. For over 20 years, the notion of self-healing concrete (SHC) being developed over time (autogenic) has been present. This can be noted in many structures and monuments that, despite having restricted maintenance, may have stayed standing for a lengthy period of time.

The observation concludes that the cracks are repaired when humidity interacts in the cracks with non-hydrated cement clinker. The first man-made self-healing process was invented in 1994, which was an artificial method of repairing cracks formed in the concrete structure The primary technique and strategy was to use a healing agent (adhesive), which is fermented inside a microcapsule; once a crack develops, the microcapsules break and start releasing the healing agent, hence starting to heal the crack. The adhesive can be preserved in short fibers or in longer tubes.

10.1.2   MAIN APPROACHES AND MECHANISM

If there is crack found in the building, it implies the loss of life span of that building structure, which is not permissible. Generally, cracks occur due to the movement of beneath foundations, landslides, vibrations, sways, and various other rationales. So, avoiding the loss of life span of structure, many approaches have been taken to create smart concrete and enhance its properties while reducing the cost of overall use of the material. Since concrete is subjected as the most dominant material in construction world, it should be treated in conventional manner, and the mechanism is used during the preparation of mortar where encapsulated balls are mixed. Furthermore, these balls are diffused when they find some crack in the structure. One of the additional or alternative methods is to mix cigarette filters/rice husk/saw dust with bacteria and adhesive, which helps to bind the two layers of cracked concrete. The application of these alternatives will result in cleaning of environment. Many of these methods were dedicated to SHC, and these methods have proved to be efficient and easy to use (Fig. 10.2).

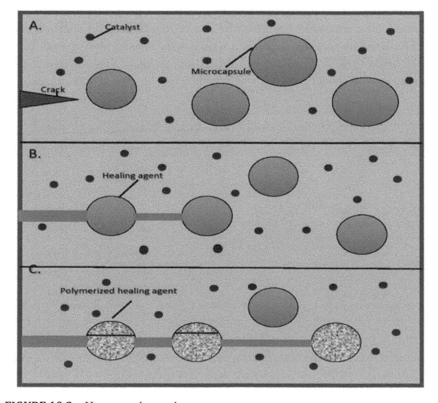

FIGURE 10.2   How capsules work.

10.1.3 BACTERIA-BASED HEALING

These are also known as the Eco-Concrete, as these types of concrete use a simple process to fill the formed crack. The main goal is achieved by making a concrete mixture that contains the bacteria planted in micro-capsules (or just added in the mixture) that will germinate once the water reaches the crack. As soon as the bacteria germinate and grow, they produce limestone ($CaCO_3$) caused by the multiplication of the bacteria. It is proved by biochemists that incorporating bacteria in concrete adds a double-layer protective shield in order to prevent corrosion in steel structure. Not to be forgotten that it emits oxygen that would then enhance the process of steel corrosion. These bacteria which are being used with concrete are spore-forming and alkali-resistant bacteria. Bacteria of this group are the almost acceptable as they are spore-forming and can live for more than 20 decades in dry circumstances. Therefore, the use of bacteria as a healing mechanism is one of the finest mechanisms to produce a concrete work because of its sustainable organic characteristics. This process is going to create a new era for construction world. It is also possible to design to have a self-healing capacity that never retards its strength (Fig. 10.3).

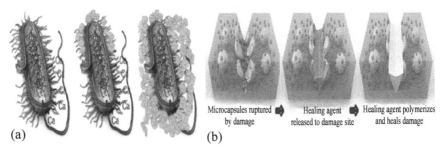

Microcapsules ruptured ➡ Healing agent ➡ Healing agent polymerizes
by damage   released to damage site   and heals damage

(a)   (b)

FIGURE 10.3   (a) Microbacteria and (b) capsulated form of bacteria.

We then classify them as autonomous materials that can be subdivided into passive and active modes again. In passive mode, the discerning material is competent of reacting to outside jolts without the requirement for human intercession, although in dynamic mode, the materials or structure needs mediation to wrap up the recuperating handle.

10.1.4 USES OF ENVIRONMENT WASTE

This process is also similar to the previous one except using of bacteria. Here, the microcapsules will be filled with cigarette filters (crushed), rice husk, and sawdust proportionally mixed with adhesive. But the most efficient and functioning will be the cigarette filters, as they are made from the cellulose acetate fiber. One of the efficient works can be done with it; rice husk and sawdust are easily biodegradable, but cigarette filters generally take 18 months to 16 years to decay. The use of these filters makes the environment clean and cannot produce harm to the nature.

The function of the acetate is to particulate the impurities phase by retention (filtration) and finely divide the carbons. These carbons which occur due to the crack formation will be absorbed by the filters and provide maximum strength to the concrete. Cigarette filters can be considered to be of the highest strength compared to other classes of compounds.

The mechanism of this process is done with the help of human intervention; when these encapsulated balls which are filled with adhesive, cigarette filters/rice husk/saw dust are used in the cracks, they start releasing the mixture into the cracks. The mixture will make its space and start to contract with the cracks over time.

10.2 PROPOSED WORK

In the previous analysis, it is mentioned that SHC materials were developed to provide strength and increase the life of concrete structures. Bacteria-based SHC was created by incorporating a microbial self-healing agent that has the ability to enhance the self-healing ability obtained primarily by mineral precipitation caused by bacteria. The method relies on bacteria that produce urease that is omnipresent in nature. The general reactions can be summarized as follows:

$$CO(NH_2)_2 + H_2O \rightarrow NH_2COOH + NH_3NH_2COOH + H_2O$$
$$\rightarrow NH3 + H_2CO_3H_2CO_3$$
$$\leftrightarrow HCO_3^- + H^+ 2NH_3 + 2H_2O$$
$$\leftrightarrow 2NH_4^+ + 2OH^-HCO_3^- + H^+ + 2NH_4^+ + 2OH$$
$$\leftrightarrow CO_3^{2-} + 2NH_4^+ + 2H_2OCa^{2+} + Cell$$
$$\rightarrow Cell - Ca^{2+}Cell - Ca^{2+} + CO_3^{2-}$$
$$\rightarrow Cell - CaCO_3^-$$

10.2.1   BACTERIA USED IN CONCRETE-

Various types of bacteria were used with construction materials. Bacillus was used on the concrete surface for calcite precipitation. The nutrients that can precipitate calcite for the bacteria are sources of calcium, phosphorous, and nitrogen. These bacterial parts stay dormant in concrete, and when water flow occurs, the bacterial element reacts to precipitate calcite with nutrient, that is, $CaCO_3$. The microbes which are utilized in concrete are as follows (Figs. 10.4 and 10.5):

- *B. sphaericus*
- *Escherichia coli*
- *Bacillus subtitles*
- *Bacillus cohnii*
- *Bacillus balodurans*
- *B. pseudofirmus*

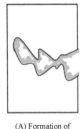   

| (A) Formation of calcium carbonate | (B) Blocking by impurities | (C) Hydration of unreacted cement | (D) Expansion of the hydrated cement |

FIGURE 10.4 (A)

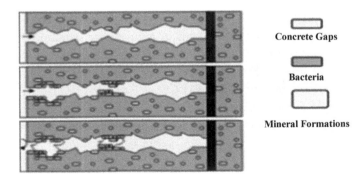

Concrete Gaps

Bacteria

Mineral Formations

FIGURE 10.4 (B)

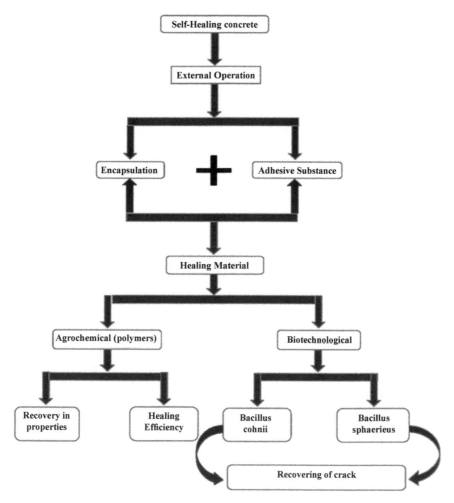

FIGURE 10.5   Schematic scenarios of self-healing by encapsulated bacteria.

10.2.2   BACTERIAL ADVANTAGES

The self-healing bacterial concrete makes it possible to maintain costs of reinforced concrete structures. Oxygen is an operator that can initiate erosion, and as microscopic organisms nourish on oxygen, propensity for the erosion of support can be decreased. Self-healing microscopic organisms can be utilized in places where human reach is troublesome for the upkeep of the structures. Subsequently it diminishes human life risk, increasing the toughness of the structure. Formation of crack will be healed in the initial stage itself, thereby increasing the service life of the structure than expected life (Fig. 10.6).

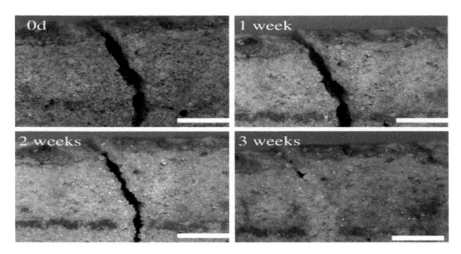

FIGURE 10.6   Showing result of 21 days of process.

10.2.3   BACTERIAL DISADVANTAGES

The cost of bacterial concrete is greater than the standard concrete. Bacteria growth in no environment and media is nice. In case the volume of self-healing agents (microscopic organisms and calcium lactate) blended gets to be more than 20%, the quality of the concrete is decreased.

10.2.4   CRACK FORMATION AND SELF-HEALING EVALUATION

Mortar cubes of size 150 mm × 150 mm × 150 mm were cast and cured in a standard curing room at a temperature of 20°C and RH of 90%. After 24 h, all samples were demolded and then stored in the same room until tests. Triplicate sets were manufactured for each group. A compressive charging program has developed cracks. A mechanical test scheme (TSY-2000) was used to perform the compressive tests. The mode of displacement control was used with loading of /min. load, while all specimens were subjected to wet–dry cycles at 20°C for 4 weeks. For one cycle, specimens were submerged for 1 h in water and then exposed to ambient conditions (20°C, RH 60%) for 11 h.

The self-healing effectiveness was evaluated as follows:

➤ **Mechanical tests:** The compressive tests were conducted using the same mechanical test system, and each specimen's compressive strength was recorded. Simultaneously cracks were made. Compressive strength was once again tested under the same circumstance after 28 days of healing. The quality recuperation proportion "r" was the compressive quality of the example after mending isolating that of the intaglio example:

$$r = \frac{R_{sh}}{R}$$

where R is the compaction force at first loading (MPa) and R_{sh} is the compaction force after self-healing (MPa) (Figs. 10.7 and 10.8).

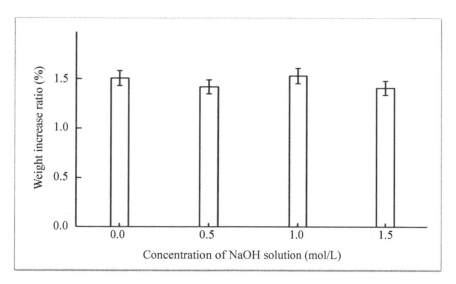

FIGURE 10.7   Stacking substance by soluble base disintegration at diverse concentrations of NaOH arrangement.

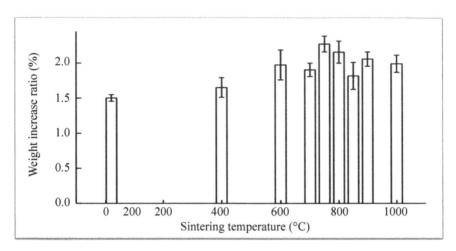

FIGURE 10.8   Loading content by heat treatment with different sintering temperatures.

➤ **Water uptake tests:** Since water absorption is one of the durability indices, the capillary water absorption test was conducted
to assess the durability after self-healing of samples. The mortar
cubes were placed in the oven at 70°C and dried between two readings at 24-h intervals until their mass loss was less than 0.1%. The
examples were at that point submerged in water at a profundity of
80±2 mm after drying. This was exhausted a 20°C environment
and a 60% RH. All examples were expelled from the water each 3
min, whereas the water level was kept up, dried with a towel on the
surface, and weighed. The samples were again submerged immediately after this measurement. Until weight stays continuous, the
operation was repeated.

➤ **Visual inspection:** Photos of the surfaces of the sample were
drawn before and after self-healing. Crack widths and healable
lengths were analyzed in each picture. The breaks can be separated
from the uncracked locale by setting a limit esteem. In this way,
the length and width of each split can be gotten. In spite of the fact
that self-healing forms containing normal and chemical are well
known to plan SHC, organic handle may be a youthful promising
innovation-, that has not been fully understood, yet many bacteria
that are helpful for the design of SHC can so far be separated from
nature.

10.2.4.1   FACTORS THAT ARE AFFECTED IN THE USE OF SELF-HEALING CONCRETE

With the use of this kind of concrete, there are many factors that interfere. As noted, as it is still under growth, it is not used in all fresh buildings. Recently, concrete based on self-healing bacteria has been effectively tested at the University of Bath in the United Kingdom on a full scale. However, the price of using it is not yet determined as it is hard to predict the net cost. The cost efficiency is one of the most valuable factors and will determine whether the material will have limited usage restricted to spots that are hard to fix and important constructions such as bridges and highways. Other than cost, long-term efficiency is one of the important factors as well alongside the size of the formed cracks that must not exceed 150 mm of depth to establish an ideal result. All in all, some factors that will definitely determine whether SHC will be used as a replacement of concrete are the economical factor, long-term efficiency, prospect suppliers, and safety factors.

10.2.4.2   ENACTMENT IN ARCHITECTURAL DESIGNS AND STRUCTURES

Because the use of SHC appears to be promising, we need to know how this will influence future architectural models. A general prognosis is difficult to make, as the building's function and size plays an enormous role in whether or not this type of concrete might be appropriate and will therefore be discussed separately.

10.2.4.3   ENACTMENT IN SMALL-SIZE AND MEDIUM-SIZED BUILDINGS (RESIDENTIAL AND PUBLIC)

Size and function of a building usually determine the approximate life span desired for this particular construction. Small-sized buildings are usually residential and located either in the suburbs, towns, or villages. And like most buildings, concrete is one of the main building materials used, especially for foundation (slabs or columns), and as small residential buildings rarely change function, it is practical to want to increase their life span and hence use SHC. Medium-sized buildings use more concrete than any other building size, unlike skyscrapers using more steel and small-sized houses using more stone or wood. However, both residential and government medium-sized structures appear to be eligible for SHC use, and particularly in government buildings as the life span rises, designs need to be flexible and simple to alter indoor room to be effective in the use of this type of concrete Therefore, instead of demolition, there will be remodeling when the service is held within the building, which in turn has a positive effect in reducing the CO_2 emission by avoiding construction.

10.2.4.4   ENACTMENT IN LARGE-SIZE BUILDINGS AND ROADS (RESIDENTIAL AND PUBLIC)

SC is especially satisfactory for bridges and street developments as they frequently involve small-sized cracks due to heavy loads and constantly need monitoring and maintenance. The use of this type of concrete will defiantly benefit all large buildings just as the infrastructure will be enhanced by providing security and durability.

10.3   DISCUSSION

Research work on SHC is still underway; many researchers are attempting distinct methods to guarantee the same result that closes cracks with minimal interference while maintaining costs at sensible prices. It is essentially much more efficient than concrete. A brief comparison of some aspects is mentioned as follows.

10.3.1   SAFETY

Although splits in SHC are simple to shut with no included costs, at the same time, the common security of a specific development is expanded. All investigations conducted so far show that the concrete picks up approximately 25% of its unique quality within the mended spot, which more than the 15% picked-up quality back when the split is fixed by the directly accessible strategies.

10.3.2   COST

It is clear that the introduction of motorway toll development by using SHC is higher; in any case, in the long-term, solid concrete is much more cost-efficient due to the support, toughness, and the long lifespan of the development.

10.3.3   DURABILITY

Bacteria-based SHC is denser and stronger than concrete, agreeing to consideration and experimentation.

10.3.4   AVAILABILITY

This type of concrete, as it is still under growth, is used on a restricted scale and is not yet commercially common. Cost and production are some of the primary barriers.

10.3.5   EFFECTS ON ARCHITECTURE AND DESIGN

By increasing the life span of a construction, architects need to reconsider design standards. A lengthy life span requires a better construction design, as architects need to take into account two primary elements of future prognosis:

i.   Potential function within a specific construction (prospective technological needs, functional change, lifestyle change, etc.)
ii. Long-term work of urban space encompassing a certain fundamental errand is to anticipate the up-and-coming needs and the current ones to plan and build a valuable, esthetic, and, more importantly, highly flexible buildings in order to be change function easily.

10.3.6   ENVIRONMENTAL IMPACT

Cement sector is one of the two largest manufacturers of carbon dioxide (CO_2) emissions that directly harm our planet. Therefore, by using SHC, the carbon dioxide emissions are decreased significantly.

10.3.6.1   IOT INTERVENTION IN MONITORING AND MAINTENANCE OF SHC-SELF HEALING CONCRETE

IoT or Internet of things is the new and most promising technology that is overtaking the entire world. The Web of things, or IoT, may be a framework of interconnected computing gadgets, mechanical and computerized machines, objects, creatures, or individuals that are given with interesting identifiers (UIDs) and the capacity to exchange data over a arrange without requiring human-to-human or human-to-computer interaction.

10.3.6.2   THE AMALGAMATION OF IOT WITH SCH PROVIDES AND INTERDISCIPLINARY PLATFORM FOR CIVIL ENGINEERING AND INFORMATION TECHNOLOGY

IoT-enabled system enables the detection of cracks using sensor and then conveys it to the municipality people or the reliable authorities. It can also be used as a data storage of construction from beginning to the end as recorded by staffs as per daily work. Keeping of data will help the authorities in prevention or making decisions easily and far early. Sanctioning of IoT will assist the authorities to receive a location-based notification about the incident. A special monitoring system enables them to remotely inspect the situation. They get all the information about the cracks remotely. After that, a proper plan of action can be designed by the team, and the cracks can be easily recovered using the self-healing methods.

The storage of all the data in cloud storage enables and secures large amount of data transmission across globe, which would help industries to globalize. The construction companies along with the IT industries could spread out their wings in the globe. Faults and issues could get international attention of technologies and intervention if required with the help of cloud data sharing.

Moreover, the IoT intervention will make the SHC more technically sound and viable for use as a commercial product which will have a surety of constant monitoring, maintenance, and repair of all kinds of cracks and faults.

10.4   CONCLUSION

In conclusion, SHC appears to be much more effective than usual concrete. It will definitely reshape the thinking and design of the architects. By comparison, we notice that it has more advantages than disadvantages and will transform concrete from an eco-harming material into an eco-friendly material because it significantly reduces CO_2 emissions. There are presently many studies that use distinct methods to generate SHC, but the most promising strategy is the bacteria-based bio-concrete due to its simplicity compared to other processes.

Meanwhile, architects need to create fresh design methods; those that enable flexibility to readily change tasks, for example, by offering mobile partitions to create larger or smaller spaces depending on present requirements.

This work is an amalgamation of different trades of engineering enabling modern concepts like IoT to make day-to-day services better and efficient. The IoT-enabled system monitors the cracks and makes it possible for the working authorities to make an immediate action plan. The cracks can be further treated by a modern form of cement that is being discussed over here, which is the self-healing cement. The self-healing cement is an added advantage to the entire system. This could open up many new prospects in the field of civil engineering that can be further combined with other allied trades like electronics and information technology.

KEYWORDS

- **IoT-enabled**
- **self-healing concrete**
- **uses of bacteria**
- **eco-friendly**
- **cementitious material**

REFERENCES

Achal, V.; Mukherjee, A. A Review of Microbial Precipitation for Sustainable Construction. *Constr. Build. Mater.* **2015,**93, 1224–1235.

de Koster, S. A. L.; Mors, R.M.; Nugteren, H.W.; Jonkers, H.M.; Meesters, G. M. H.; van Ommen, J. R. Geopolymer Coating of Bacteria-Containing Granules for Use in Self-Healing Concrete. *Procedia Eng.* **2015,***102*, 475–484.

De Muynck, W.; De Belie, N.; Verstraete, W. Microbial Carbonate Precipitation in Construction Materials: A Review. *Ecol. Eng.* **2010,***36*(2), 118–136.

Huang, H. L.; Ye, G.; Qian, C. X.; Schlangen, E. Self-Healing in Cementitious Materials: Materials, Methods and Service Conditions. *Mater. Design* **2016,***92*, 499–511.

Jonkers, H. M.; Thijssen, A.; Muyzer, G.; Copuroglu, O.; Schlangen, E. Application of Bacteria as Self-Healing Agent for the Development of Sustainable Concrete. *Ecol. Eng.* **2010,***36*(2), 230–235.

Li, V. C.; Herbert, E. Robust Self-Healing Concrete for Sustainable Infrastructure. *J. Adv. Concr. Technol.* **2012,***10*(6), 207–218.

Sahmaran, M.; Keskin, S. B.; Ozerkan, G.; Yaman, I. O. Self-Healing of Mechanically-Loaded Self-Consolidating Concretes with High Volumes of Fly Ash. *Cem. Concr. Compos.* **2008,***30*(10), 872–879.

Seifan, M.; Samani, A. K.; Berenjian, A. Bio Concrete: Next Generation of Self-Healing Concrete. *Appl. Microbiol. Biotechnol.* **2016,***100*(6), 2591–2602.

Siddique, R.; Chahal, N. K. Effect of Uratolytic Bacteria on Concrete Properties. *Constr. Build. Mater.* **2011,***25*(10), 3791–3801.

Wang, J. Y.; De Belie, N.; Verstraete, W. Diatomaceous Earth as a Protective Vehicle for Bacteria Applied for Self-Healing Concrete. *J. Ind. Microbiol. Biotechnol.* **2012,***39*(4), 567–577.

Wang, J. Y.; Ersan, Y. C.; Boon, N.; De Belie, N. Application of Microorganisms in Concrete: A Promising Sustainable Strategy to Improve Concrete Durability. *Appl. Microbiol. Biotechnol.* **2016,***100*(7), 2993–3007.

Wang, J. Y.; Soens, H.; Verstraete, W.; De Belie, N. Self-healing Concrete by Use of Microencapsulated Bacterial Spores. *Cem. Concr. Res.* **2014,***56*, 139–152.

Wiktor, V.; Jonkers, H. M. Quantification of Crack Healing in Novel Bacteria-Based Self-Healing Concrete. *Cem. Concr. Compos.* **2011,***33*(7), 763–770.

Wong, L. S. Microbial Cementation of Uratolytic Bacteria from the Genus Bacillus: A Review of the Bacterial Application on Cement-Based Materials for Cleaner Production. *J. Clean. Prod.* **2015,***93*, 5–17.

Wu, M.; Johannesson, B.; Geiker, M. A Review: Self-Healing in Cementitious Materials and Engineered Cementitious Composite as a Self-Healing Material. *Constr. Build. Mater.* **2012,***28*(1), 571–583.

Xu, J.; Du, Y.; Jiang, Z.; She, A. Effects of Calcium Source on Biochemical Properties of Microbial $CaCO_3$ Precipitation. *Front. Microbiol.* **2015,***6*, 1–7.

Xu, J.; Yao, W. Multiscale Mechanical Quantification of Self-Healing Concrete Incorporating Non-Uratolytic Bacteria-Based Healing Agent. *Cem. Concr. Res.* **2014,***64*(1), 1–10.

Xu, J.; Yao, W.; Jiang, Z. W. Non-Uratolytic Bacterial Carbonate Precipitation as a Surface Treatment Strategy on Cementitious Materials. *J. Mater. Civ. Eng.* **2014,***26*(5), 983–991.

Zhang, J. L.; Mai, B. X.; Cai, T. W. et al. Optimization of a Binary Concrete Crack Self-Healing System Containing Bacteria and Oxygen. *Materials* **2017,***10*(2), 116.

Zhang, J.; Liu, Y.; Feng, T. et al. Immobilizing Bacteria in Expanded Perlite for the Crack Self-healing in Concrete. *Constr. Build. Mater.* **2017,***148*, 610–617.

CHAPTER 11

IoT-Enabled Trash the Ash (TRAS): Maneuver of Salt (NaCl)

ABHINAV SINGH[1*], MEKHLA SEN[2], and RAJDEEP CHOWDHURY[3]

[1]Department of Pharmaceutical Technology, NSHM Knowledge Campus, Tollygunge, Kolkata 700053, West Bengal, India

[2]Department of Electrical Engineering, Meghnad Saha Institute of Technology, Nazirabad Road, Kolkata 700150, West Bengal, India

[3]Chinsurah, Hooghly, West Bengal, India

*Corresponding author. E-mail: abhinavsinghnshm@gmail.com

ABSTRACT

Smoking, a threat to human life, has become a serious concern. Around 120 million smokers are currently in India. As demonstrated by the World Health Organization (WHO), India is nation to 12% of the world's smokers. More than 10 million kick the bucket every year because of tobacco smoking in India. As per a 2002 WHO gauge, 70% of grown-up guys in India smoke today. Although it is very hard to quit smoking because it seems to be a one-way trap as interviewed by the adults in our country, various medications that are available in the market today initiate to cease the smoking rate of an individual, but either of them is not properly upheld. The reason behind this is because of their expenses or their bitter taste. Our product is going to cut down all these and giving us a standard base for initiating this work. Our idea is all surrounding a table salt. A pinch of table salt when licked by the tip of the tongue ceases the smoking urge. This can be implemented in day-to-day life within the frame of tablets as rapid dissolving tablets which when placed in the sublingual cavity of our mouth would dissolve rapidly without chewing it. Although it may not help out with complete cessation from smoking but rather can decrease the rate of smoking in an individual. Collectively, it could be taken many times in a day within a permissible limit, having no side effects as well as the bitter taste which the either ones have. This product may receive a great market acceptance because of its economic factor and the most important fact is all about side effects. It would contain the strip of 10 tablets and would cost much lesser than a cost of a cigarette.

11.1 INTRODUCTION

It is not new to anybody that smoking is a well-being risk; however, numerous individuals disregard the peril and keep smoking. Albeit a few smokers are willfully ignorant about the dangers related to smoking, most of the smokers continue in light of the truth that it is difficult to cease. Numerous smokers are truly dependent on nicotine and think that it is simpler to proceed with the propensity than to attempt to stop.

It is the addictive nature of nicotine that makes ceasing smoking so troublesome. Smoking is the foremost broadly recognized word among us today. Smoking may be a difficult penchant to break as tobacco contains nicotine, which is especially addictive. Like heroin or other addictive medicines, the body and mind quickly become so addicted to the nicotine in cigarettes that a person has to have it fair to feel ordinary. People begin smoking for several reasons. In the previous times of smoking, a Frenchman named Jean Nicot (from whose name, the word nicotine determines) acquainted tobacco with France in 1560 from Spain. From that point, it spread to England. The primary report of a smoking Englishman is of a mariner in Bristol in 1556, seen "discharging smoke from his noses."

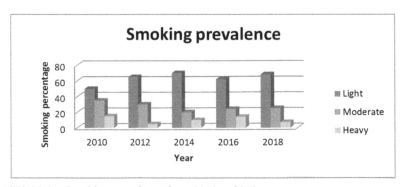

GRAPH 11.1   Smoking prevalence from 2010 to 2018.

The historical backdrop of smoking goes back to as right on time as 5000 B.C. in the Americas in shamanistic customs. With the entry of the Europeans in the 16th century, the utilization, development, and exchanging of tobacco rapidly spread. The modernization of cultivating hardware and assembling expanded the accessibility of cigarettes following the reproduction time in the United States (Graph 11.1).

Large-scale manufacturing immediately extended the extent of utilization, which developed until the logical discussions of the 1960s and judgment during the 1980s. A survey conveyed that smoking individuals are around 120 million in India. As indicated by a 2002 WHO gauge, 70% of grown-up guys in India smoke. Among grown-up females, the figure is much lower at between 13 and 15%.

About 90% of youngsters younger than 16 years (10th class) have utilized some type of tobacco previously, and 70% are as yet utilizing tobacco items. Change begins with a test. The vast majority quit smoking since life presents them with a challenge to their smoking propensity. Maybe they wind up hacking and wheezing after exercise that never disturbed them, or they see a friend or family amazing smoking-related lung malignancy (Fig. 11.1).

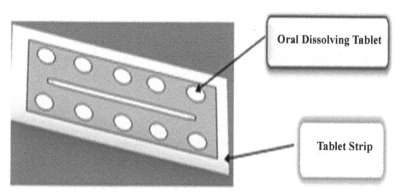

Oral Dissolving Tablet

Tablet Strip

FIGURE 11.1 Tablet strips of oral dissolving tablet.

Perhaps, they take a gander at their youngsters and they understand that they probably will not live to see them arrive at adulthood on the off-chance that they keep on smoking. Any condition that makes you question whether you should keep on smoking can turn into the test that starts you making progress toward stopping. Individuals who endeavor to stop smoking in any case bomb regularly on the grounds that they did not have an arrangement for confronting allurements (Fig. 11.2).

Bitter

Sour

Salty

Sweet

FIGURE 11.2   Buds of tongue showing different tastes.

Perhaps, they started a program but felt pressured to smoke in social situations or they found an old pack and decided there was no harm in smoking just one. The most important thing you can do for yourself as you prepare to quit is to decide how you are going to face similar temptations in your own life. Deciding on a plan and sticking to it will ensure that you are successfully moving toward your goal.

So, this chapter is basically confined with the aim to quit smoking with the help of an easy and pocket-friendly way (Fig. 11.3).

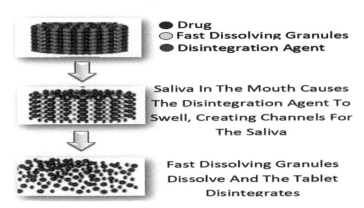

FIGURE 11.3   Drug-release contrivance.

11.2   LITERATURE REVIEW

It is the solution, very difficult to quit, one goes deeper and deeper. As expressed worldwide, benefits of tobacco exchange add up to $35 bn as smokers passed the 6 million mark. Revenues from worldwide tobacco deals are assessed to be near to $500 bn, creating combined benefits for the six biggest firms of $35.1 bn—more than $1100 a moment. There are different compositions of medication accessible in advertisements nowadays, which costs much as well as have an awfully sharp taste. The different compositions accessible are described in the following.

11.2.1   BUPROPION

It was actually approved as an antidepressant intending immediate release and extended release.

The mechanism of action of this drug is that it works by hindering the reuptake of the brain chemicals noradrenaline and dopamine that are direct acting sympathetic. This drug has shown growth rates in smoking cessation.

11.2.2   VARENICLINE

It helps to reduce nicotine cravings by stimulating the alpha-4 beta-2 nicotinic receptor but much lesser content than nicotine.

Marketed products available are as follows:

➤   Nicotex (Cipla)
➤   Sudarshan Ayurveda Nasha Muktam (Ayurvedic medicine)
➤   Chantix
➤   Nicotine lozenges

All these products are much expensive and have a very bitter taste. In comparison with these products, we are coming up with a very much economic, safe as well as easily available product, rather to say a home remedy for decreasing the rate of smoking by an individual.

11.3   PROPOSED WORK

The proposed idea is that if a pinch of salt is taken and licked at the tip of the tongue, it decreases the urge of smoking for an hour. So, this can be made available in day-to-day life of a smoking individual in the form of tablets. This tablet would contain salt as its active pharmaceutical ingredient along with the excipients such as dummy powders, lactose, and sucrose (Fig. 11.4).

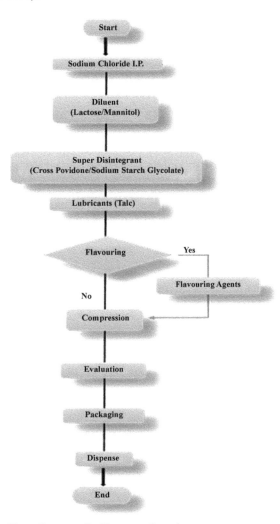

FIGURE 11.4   Flow diagram of tablet manufacturing process.

This composition would have many advantages such as no side effects and easily available, and the most important thing about this composition would be that it will be a rapid dissolving tablet (RDT) that can be placed under the tongue and would dissolve rapidly without chewing. The disintegration time given as per Indian Pharmacopoeia is 10 s for an RDT. So, this tablet would be easily available, easy to take, having the simplest route of administration. The most important fact is that a strip of 10 tablets would cost much lesser than the cost of a cigarette (Fig. 11.5).

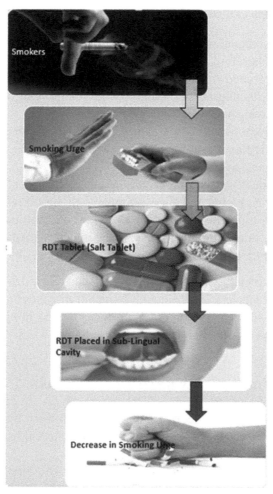

FIGURE 11.5   Working of TRAS.

11.4   VISIONS FOR THE FUTURE

It is hard to quit smoking because the nicotine in cigarettes, cigars, and other tobacco products gets you hooked and keeps you hooked. Since smoking discontinuance can be an incredibly troublesome procedure, seeing precisely how smoking damages your body can help keep you persuaded to kick the propensity.

The abovementioned proposed medicine provides a brief synopsis of the dangers related to smoking, as it will help to reduce the urge of smoking cigarettes to a huge extent.

> ➤ As the medicine will be made of table salt, so it will have no side effects. Therefore, it can be consumed as required.
> ➤ The researched medicine will be characterized with RDT agent that will disintegrate or dissolve rapidly on tongue within seconds with chewing and water.
> ➤ It will have a fresh flavoring agent to avoid the bitter and medicinal taste. This flavor would enhance, modify the taste and aroma, so that people can easily take it.
> ➤ This product will be in the form of tablets or capsules that would rate very economical; hence, people would buy it with even lower cost than cigarettes. Therefore, keeping all the abovementioned points in mind, there is an assurance that this medicine can be a cease solution to the increasing rate of smoking.

It cannot completely kick this bad habit but can minimize it to adequate level. So, to stop accelerating the development of diseases due to addiction to smoking, we have to take immediate measures to implementing the production rate of this medicine in extreme amount.

11.4.1   IOT INTERVENTION WITH TRASH THE ASH

The amalgamation of Internet of things (IoT) with trash the ash (TRAS) provides an interdisciplinary platform for pharmaceutical background and information technology.

IoT-enabled TRAS, rather say, will determine the number of tablets you would have with you per day in order to cease the smoking urge. IoT-enabled cloud storage will also provide the number of smoker individuals and thus weighing the comparison between the smokers and the ones who have used this tablet leading to the cessation of smoking.

The storage of all the data in cloud storage enables secured and large amount of data transmission across the globe that would help industries to globalize. This IoT system can also be integrated as an application that would suggest you to take as of daily. This would also help an individual to check themselves in contrast to a number of cigarettes would have smoke to the latter one and also the decrease in carboxyhemoglobin level, heart rate, money-saving, etc.

Moreover, the IoT intervention will make the TRAS more pharmaceutically sound and viable for use as a commercial product that will have a surety of constant monitoring, regular feedbacks, and the betterment of an individual.

11.5 CONCLUSION

Cigarette smoking by youth and youthful grown-ups has quick antagonistic well-being outcomes, including fixation, and quickens the improvement of interminable illnesses over the full life course. The proposed work is sufficient to conclude that the medicine composed of table salt can diminish the trigger of smoking to maximum extent.

Hence, this medicine needs to be fast popular in the market so that people can know about its advantages and use it to kick out this bad habit of smoking in a very cheap, safe, and healthy way.

KEYWORDS

- **cease smoking urge**
- **cost-effective tablets**
- **rapid onset of action**
- **easily available**

REFERENCES

Agaku, I. T.; King, B. A.; Husten, C. G. et al. Tobacco Product Use Among Adults—United States, 2012–2013. *MMWR Morb. Mortal. Wkly. Rep.* **2014,** *63* (25), 542–547.

Center for Behavioral Health Statistics and Quality. *Results from the 2016 National Survey on Drug Use and Health: Detailed Tables*; SAMHSA: Rockville, MD, 2017. https://www.samhsa.gov/data/sites/default/files/NSDUH-DetTabs-2016/NSDUH-DetTabs-2016.pdf (accessed Sept 14, 2017).

Cook, B. L.; Wayne, G. F.; Kafali, E. N.; Liu, Z.; Shu, C.; Flores, M. Trends in Smoking Among Adults with Mental Illness and Association Between Mental Health Treatment and Smoking Cessation. *JAMA* **2014,** *311* (2), 172–182. DOI:10.1001/jama.2013.284985.

Jamonno Curnt Cigareng Adults—United States, 2005–2014. *MMWR. Morb. Mortal. Wkly. Rep.* **2015,** *64* (44), 1233–1240. DOI: 10.15585/mmwr.mm6444a2.

Kollins, S. H.; Adcock, R. A. ADHD, Altered Dopamine Neurotransmission, and Disrupted Reinforcement Processes: Implications for Smoking and Nicotine Dependence. *Prog. Neuropsychopharmacol. Biol. Psychiatry* **2014,** *52,* 70–78. DOI: 10.1016/j.pnpbp.2014.02.002.

Mantey, D. S.; Cooper, M. R.; Clendennen, S, L.; Pasch, K. E.; Perry, C. L. E-Cigarette Marketing Exposure Is Associated with E-Cigarette Use Among US Youth. *J. Adolesc. Health* **2016,** *58* (6), 686–690. DOI: 10.1016/j.jadohealth.2016.03.003.

Miechnston, L.; Bac, P.; *Patrick Monitoring the Future National Adolescent Drug Trends in 2017: Findings Released*; Institute for Social Research, The University of Michigan: Ann Arbor, MI, 2017. http://www.monitoringthefuture.org//pressreleases/17drugpr.pdf (accessed Jan 2, 2018).

National Center for Chronic Disease Prevention and Health Promotion (US) Office on Smoking and Health. *The Health Consequences of Smoking—50 Years of Progress: A Report of the Surgeon General*; Centers for Disease Control and Prevention, US: Atlanta, GA, 2014. http://www.ncbi.nlm.nih.gov/books/NBK179276/

National Center for Health Statistics. *National Health Interview Survey, 1997–2016*; Centers for Disease Control and Prevention, 2017. https://www.cdc.gov/nchs/data/nhis/earlyrelease/earlyrelease201705_08.pdf (accessed Sept 14, 2017).

Roberts, M. E.; Doogan, N. J.; Kurti, A. N. et al. Rural Tobacco Use Across the United States: How Rural and Urban Areas Differ, Broken Down by Census Regions and Divisions. *Health Place* **2016,** *39,* 153–159. DOI: 10.1016/j.healthplace.2016.04.001.

Singh, T.; Arrazola, R. A.; Corey, C. G. et al. Tobacco Use Among Middle and High School Students—United States, 2011–2015. *MMWR Morb. Mortal. Wkly. Rep.* **2016,** *65* (14), 361–367. DOI: 10.15585/mmwr.mm6514a1.

Smith, P. H.; Mazure, C. M.; McKee, S. A. Smoking and Mental Illness in the U.S. Population. *Tob. Control* **2014,** *23* (e2), e147–e153. DOI: 10.1136/tobaccocontrol-2013-051466.

Stanton, C. A.; Keith, D. R.; Gaalema, D. E. et al. Trends in Tobacco Use Among US Adults with Chronic Health Conditions: National Survey on Drug Use and Health 2005–2013. *Prev. Med.* **2016,** *92,* 160–168. DOI: 10.1016/j.ypmed.2016.04.008.

Substance Abuse and Mental Health Services Administration. *Adults with Mental Illness of Substance Use Disorder Account for 40 Percent of All Cigarettes Smoked*; SAMHSA: Rockville, MD, 2013. https://www.samhsa.gov/data/sites/default/files/spot104-cigarettes-mental-illness-substance-use-disorder/spot104-cigarettes-mental-illness-substance-use-disorder.pdf (accessed Oct 6, 2017).

Warner, K. E. Frequency of E-Cigarette Use and Cigarette Smoking by American Students in 2014. *Am. J. Prev. Med.* **2016,** *51* (2), 179–184. DOI: 10.1016/j.amepre.2015.12.004.

Index